Walk With Me...

In the Garden of Our Friendship

NAN RAE

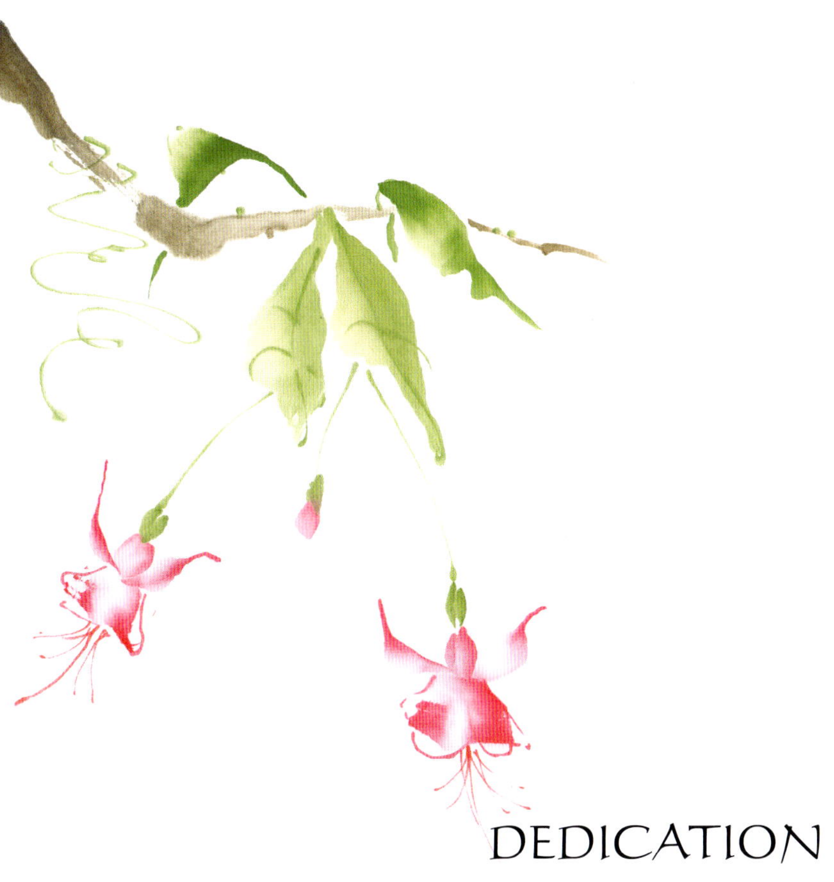

DEDICATION

To all those who go forth in the world with loving kindness, speaking the unforced rhythms of Grace.

Cover art: Nan Rae: An Exciting Day
Text set in Shelley Volante BT, Calligraphic 421, Zapfino and Minion Pro

A joint production of Nan Rae Studio and Laughing Elephant Books

First published in 2022 by
LAUGHING ELEPHANT BOOKS
PO Box 632871
San Diego, CA 92163

LAUGHINGELEPHANTBOOKS.com

First printing 2022

Printed in China

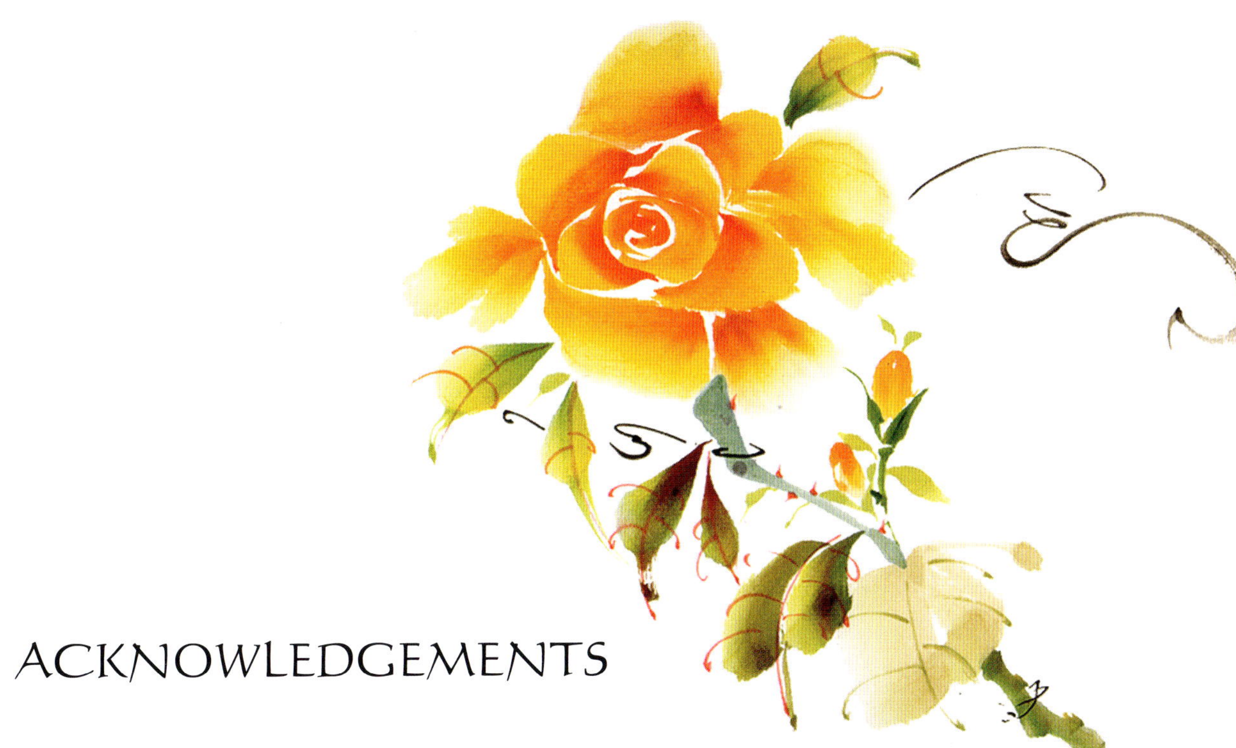

ACKNOWLEDGEMENTS

For this little book I have to acknowledge the faith that my mother always had in me, even when I exhibited no basis in reality for it. When I was older, she reflected that she always knew I would flower and truly become my own person. It's been quite a journey getting there, but thanking my mother was perhaps the first step.

Special thanks have to go to my most literate and kind author friend Carol Soucek King for asking me to present the monthly Meditations for her "Salon on the Spiritually Creative Life." These Meditations are based on the ten topics in her book, "Under the Bridges at Arroyo del Rey," which further developed lectures given in the Salon based on the Spiritually Creative Life.

As always, Veronica Carrasco, the best associate one could hope for, brought my thoughts all together to create this book you now hold in your hands. Thank you to Benjamin Darling at Laughing Elephant Books, my publisher extraordinaire, for once again saying yes to me.

Since so many more of my words are contained in these pages, dear Lucia Moskal opened her heart yet again to brilliantly edit my ramblings.

My thanks to everyone who opened a door to me and even more to those who closed one as that is where I really grew.

INTRODUCTION

From the beginning, along with my publisher Benjamin Darling at Laughing Elephant Books, three books were envisioned to fully express my journey through life. "What If…We Have the Power to Change Our Lives" was shorthand notes to describe fully embracing our lives in a powerful, loving way, and "That's Just What I Needed Today" added to my thoughts by sharing wisdom from the world's most inspirational thinkers.

Book three stopped me completely. Wanting the same format of brief thoughts accompanied by my artwork, I was stymied. What I usually wind up saying whenever I'm stuck is to just get over yourself, and saying that worked well here as I was then able to put on paper the thinking that has framed my life and strengthened my journey. Along the way, my dear friend Carol Soucek King suggested I include the Meditations that I read each month for her "Salon on the Spiritually Creative Life." The more I thought about that, the more I realized that throughout the year, writing these Meditations helped me to bring into focus my thoughts about how best to go forward in life, and so they will be included in these pages. My hope is that in reading these pages you will be empowered, knowing that every word expressed here has been tested by fire and proven true!

This is perhaps the strangest time I have ever lived through… not just for me but for the world.

Two years ago I was telling everyone that only the strong would survive, and now it appears it's a time of great testing and also of great rewards. I feel I'm guided in such little ways that I'm reminded again of my strong belief that our Creator is interested in the smallest details of our lives. Having faith in this makes us strong.

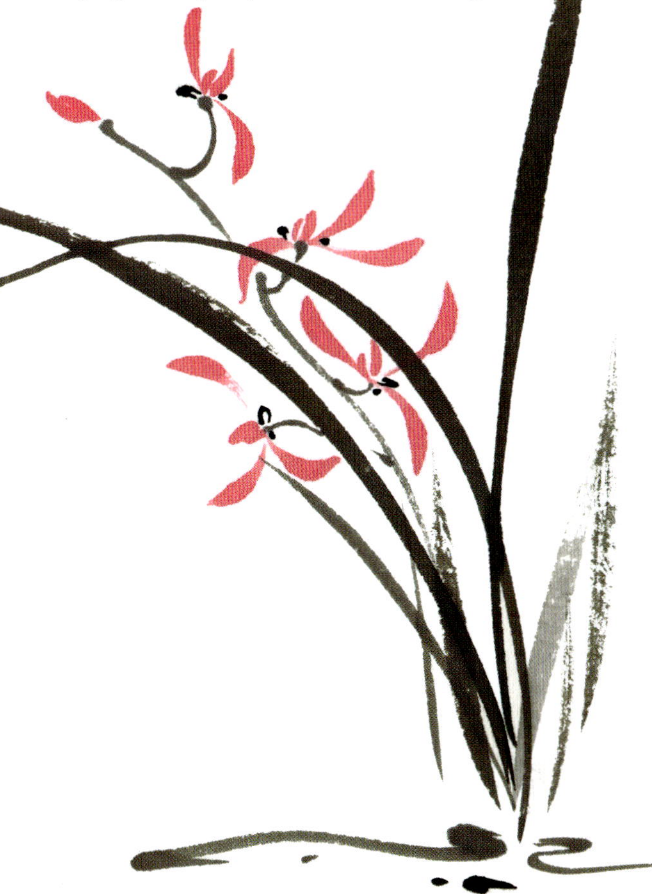

Many years ago, I went with a friend to the beautiful Saint Sophia's church in Los Angeles designed on the original Hagia Sophia in Constantinople and built by Charles Skouras, the head of 20th Century Fox, who vowed to God he would do it if he became successful in the movie business. While the outside is a simplified Byzantine Revival, the interior is over-the-top Hollywood decorative glamour.

At the back of the church written on an archway is a quote from the Minnie Louise Haskins poem, "The Gate of the Year," written in 1908 and first quoted by King George VI in his 1939 Christmas broadcast to give hope to his people. It has been used and quoted many times since, and seeing it... feeling it... was a guiding North Star throughout my life.

("And I said to the man who stood at the gate of the year:
"Give me a light that I may tread safely into the unknown."
And he replied:)

"Go out into the darkness and
put your hand into the Hand of God.
That shall be to you
better than light and safer
than a known way."

I've learned to *accept* what is and see
how it can be even better than what was and to see
the *great gift of every friendship,*
to *treasure every precious moment,*
to *consider the marvel of our planet* and
the space we've been allowed to inhabit.

Perhaps the greatest secret to stability is
beginning and ending each day with gratitude,
real soul-searching gratitude,
understanding the gift of being here and
the countless people and events who have helped along the way.
I now ask to have
eyes to see all the good that's in my life
and a heart that is receptive.
to the yes that we must all hear.

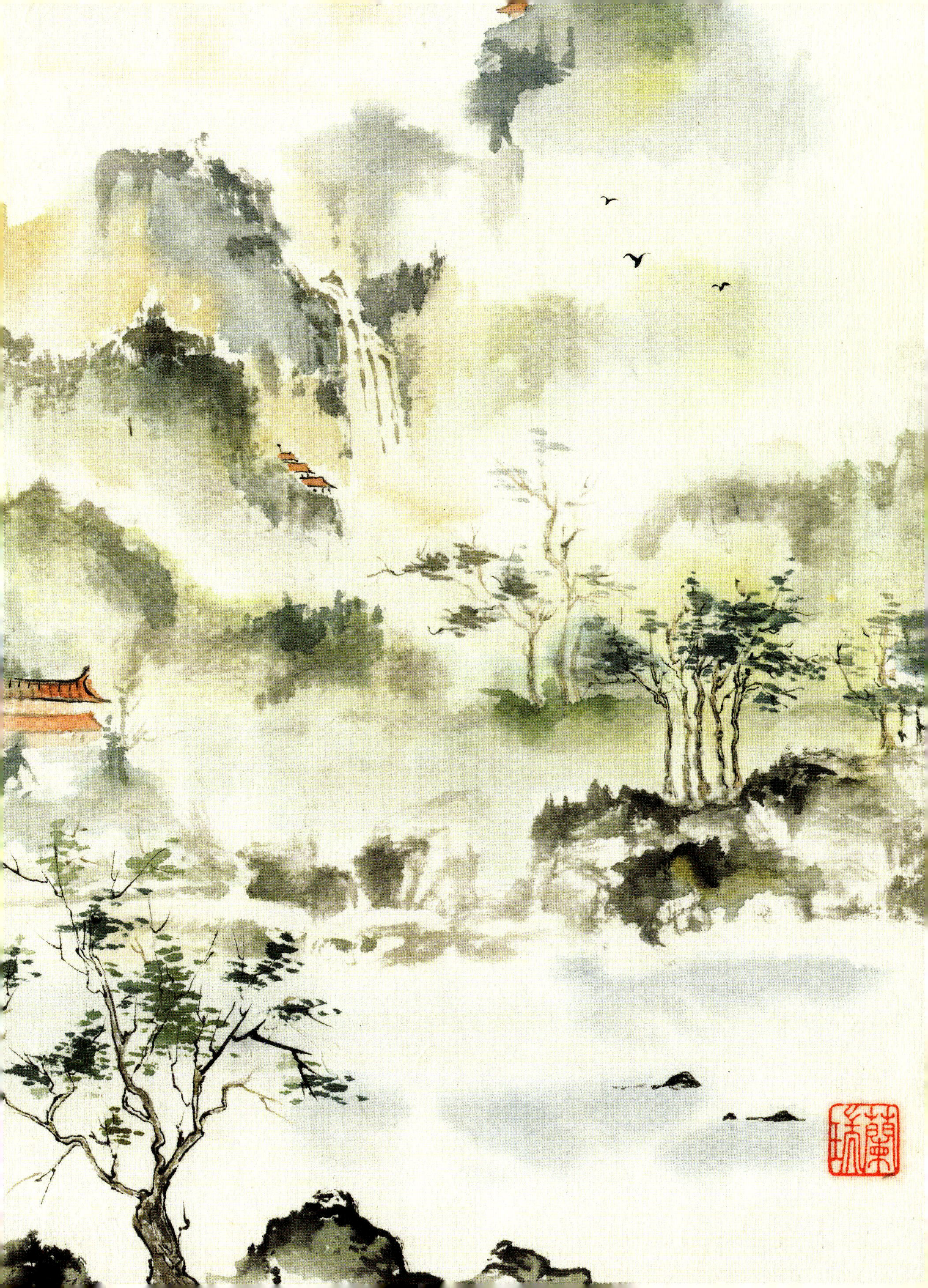

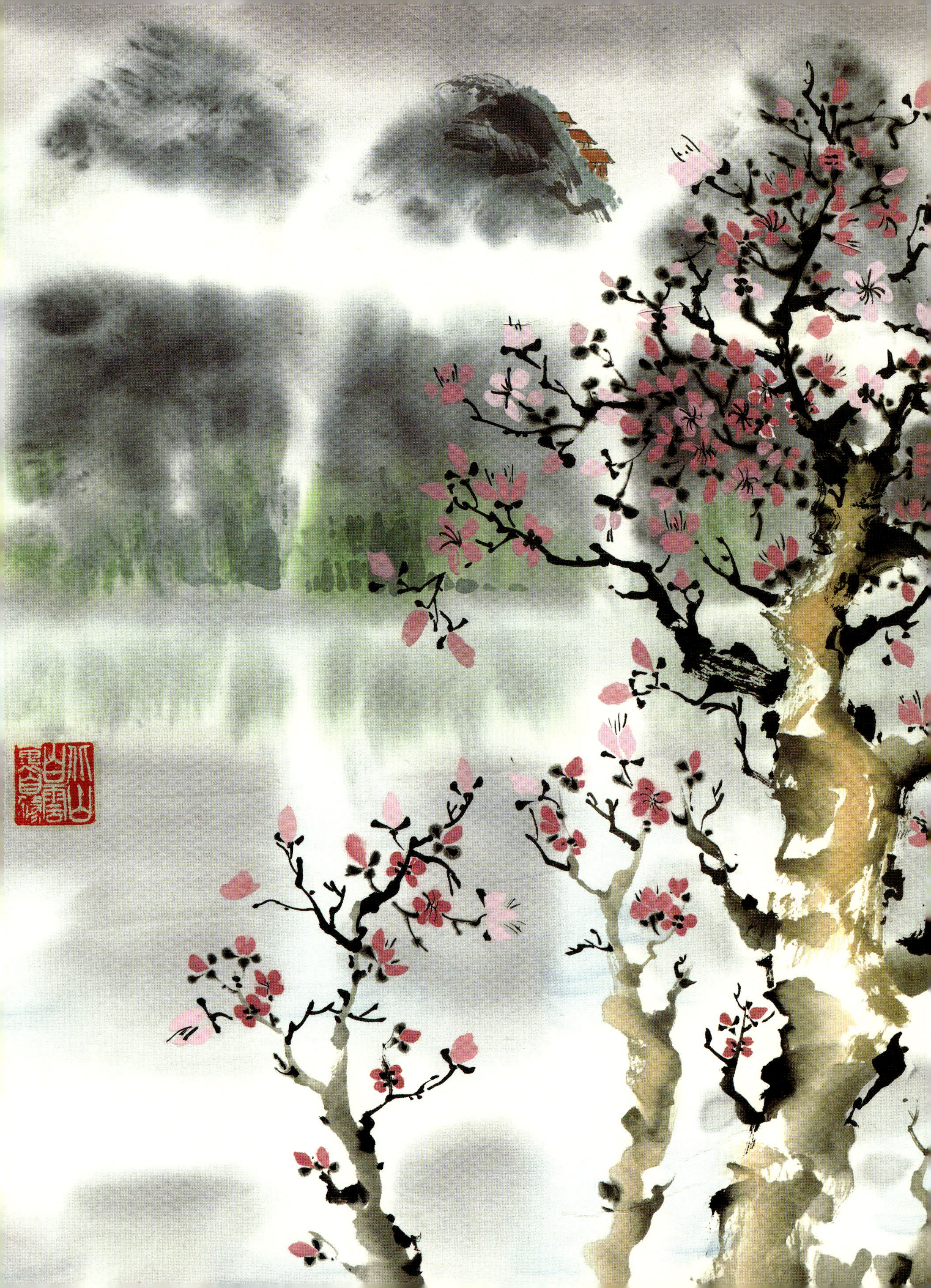

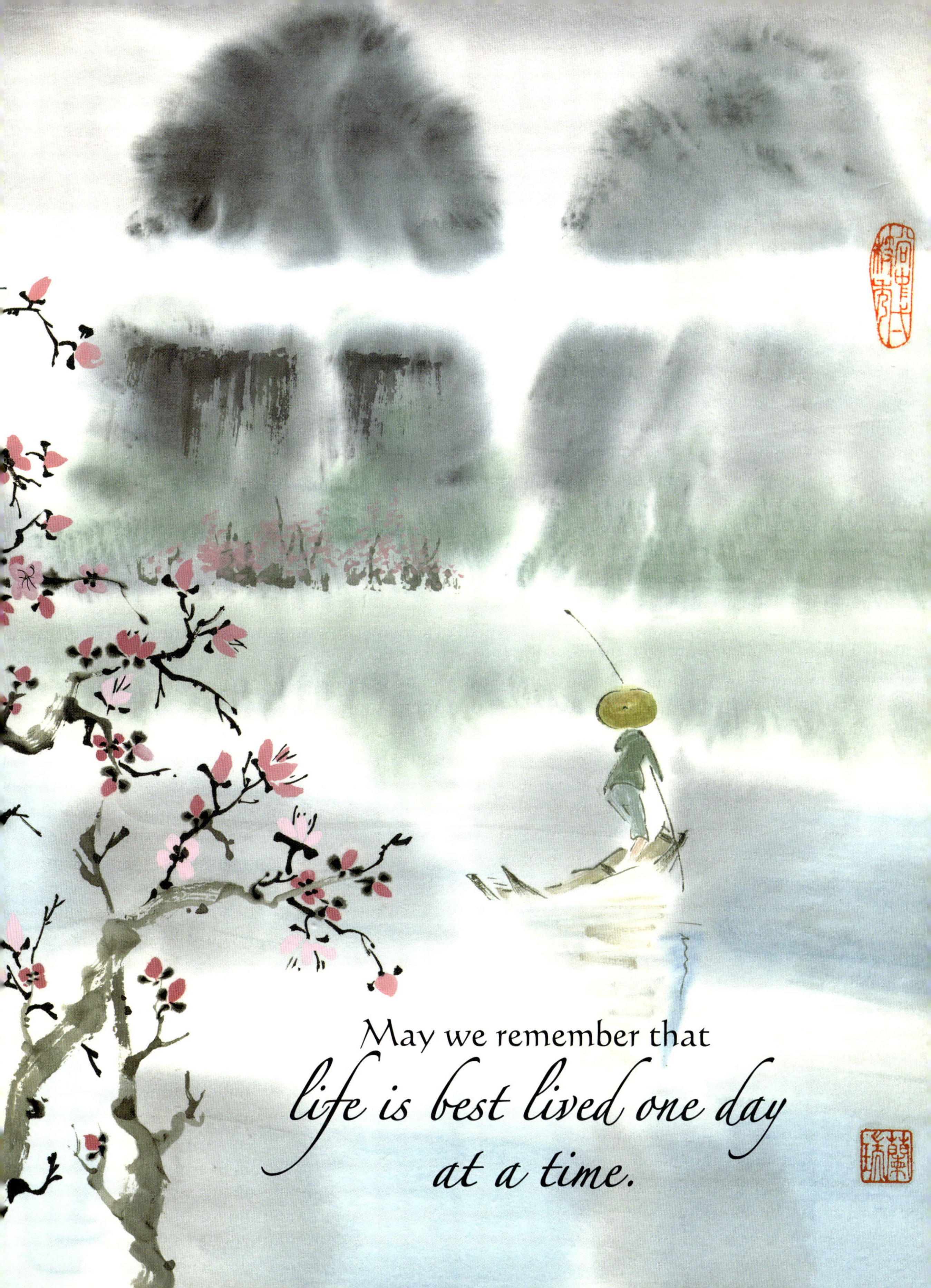
May we remember that
life is best lived one day
at a time.

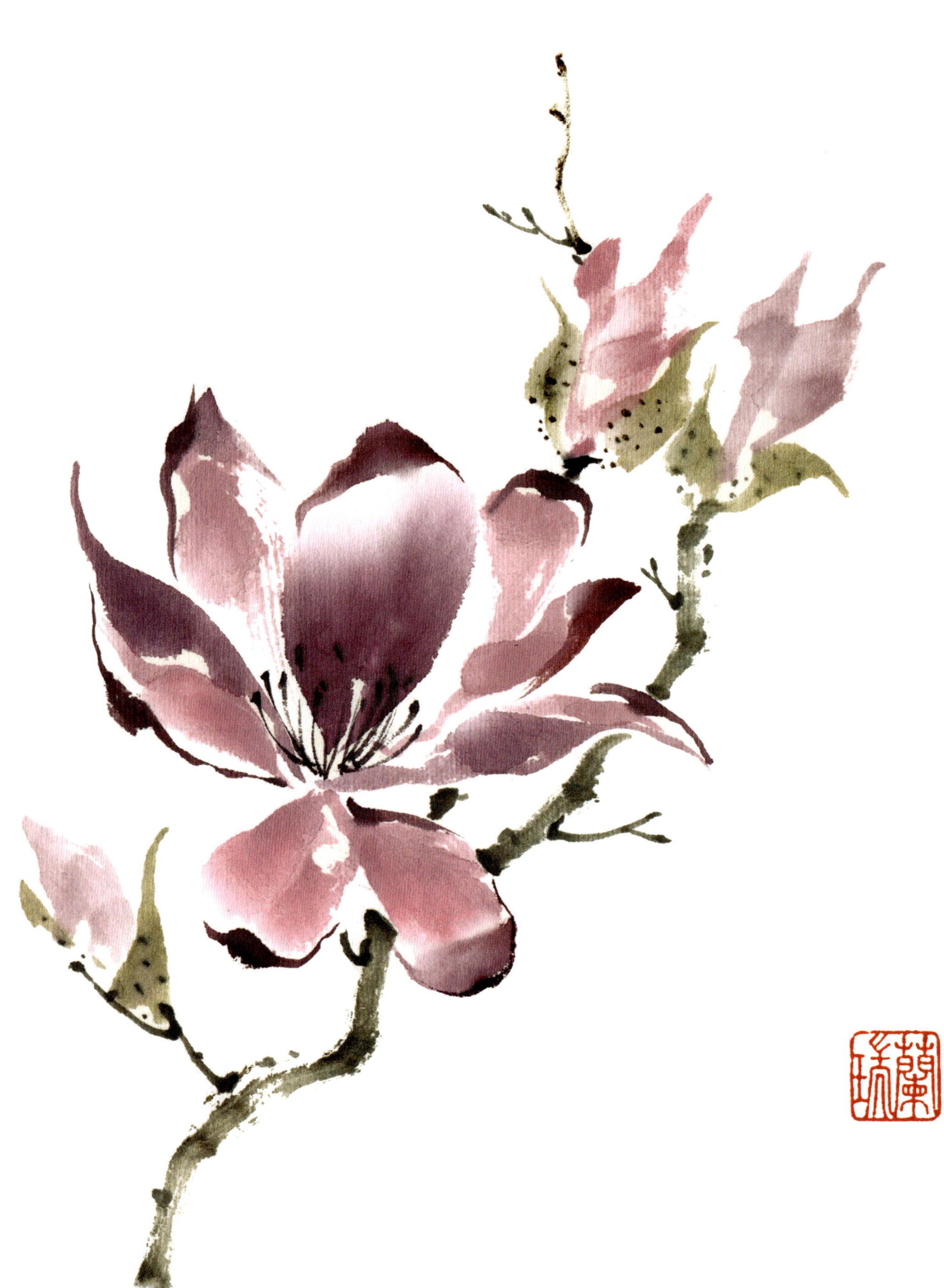

MEDITATION ON

Growth

Resolving to daily express gratitude and be intentionally kind has
made me mindful in each moment to what is required of me in every
encounter whether it be in person,
on the phone, e-mail or social media.
I clearly see that *KIND* is a verb and
almost always requires action albeit large or small.

Everything must grow and I think about that as
I mindfully enter my little garden, read books about trees, birds and
plants and watch inspiring nature documentaries.
Now, just as Ray Bradbury,
I'm consistently and intentionally doing what I love.
Hank Aaron said, "I recognized that I had a gift."

For the first time I finally see the *gift* I've been given as my purpose,
my obligation, my way of accounting for the space I'm inhabiting.
How wonderful if we could *see and love our purpose*
and along with that make kindness our larger purpose,
discovering that the best way to be in this *kindness flow*
is to always obey/follow through a good impulse.
May we always grow.

The sun is shining…
I am *grateful*.
The earth is spinning…
I am not.
The garden's *growing*
and I am too!

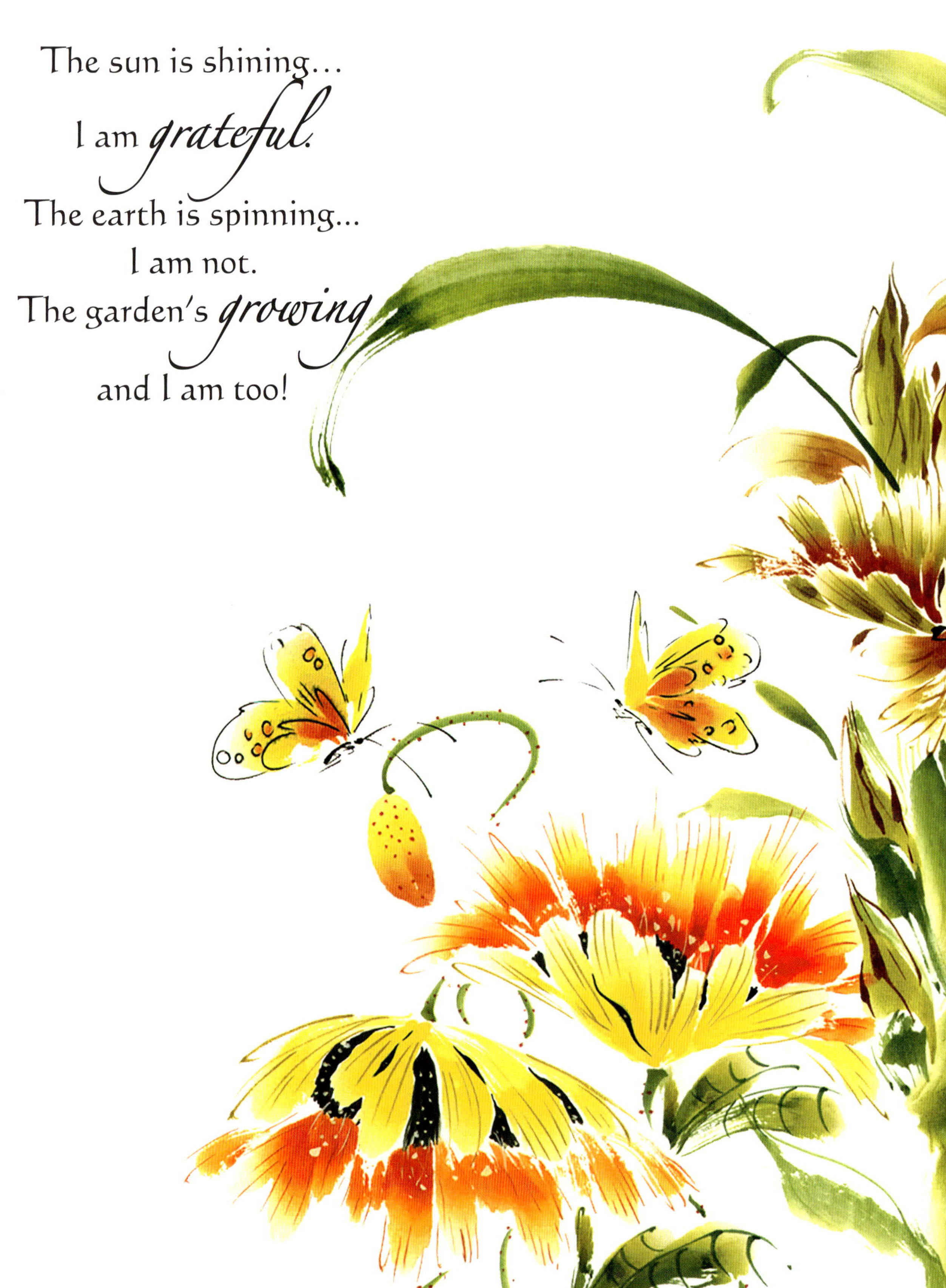

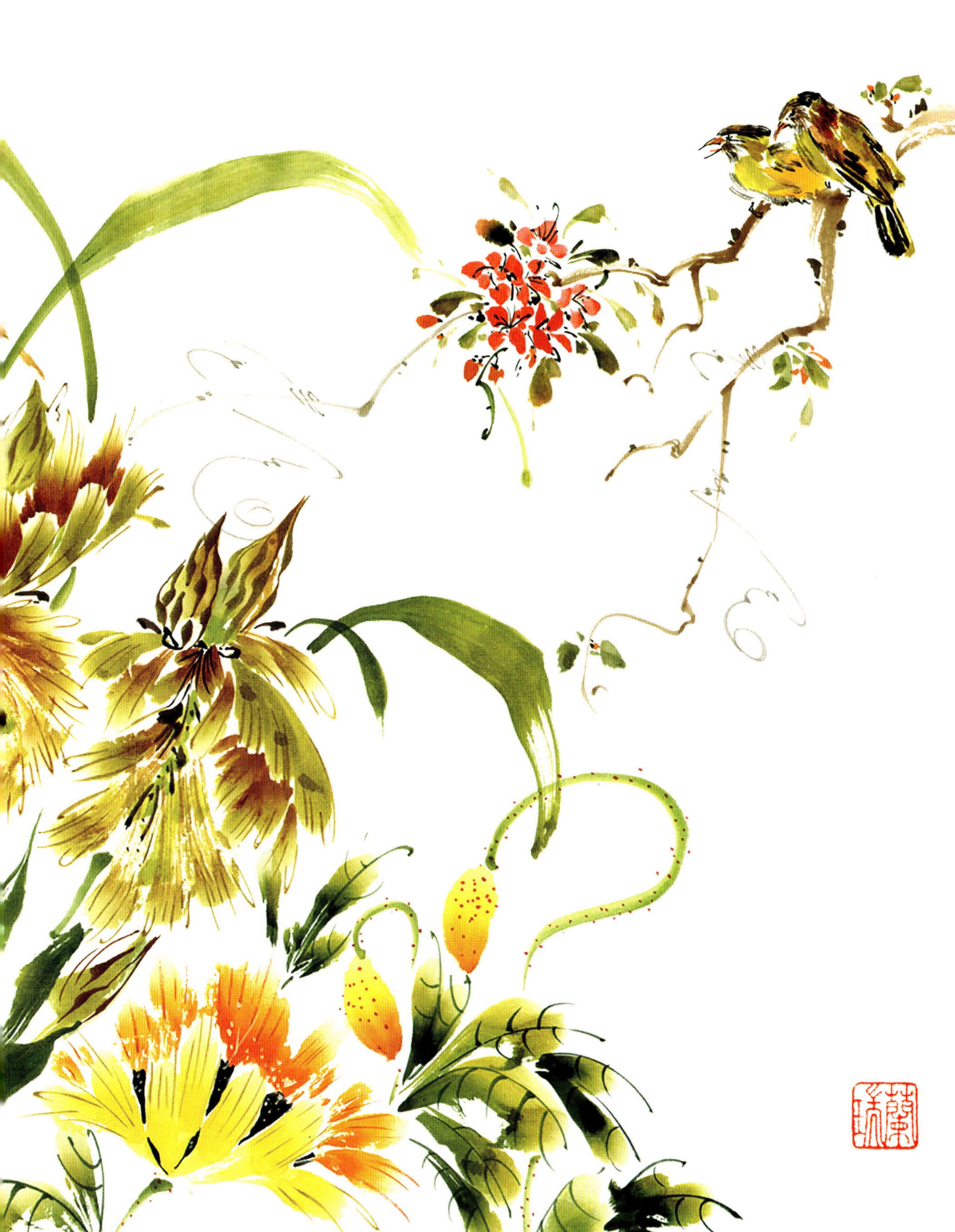

MEDITATION ON
Possibility

Do we understand possibility?
There are strings that keep us tethered,
never experiencing all that
would be possible for us.
My artwork was used in a very special little book,
"Suma the Elephant," by Gary Shoup.
For SUMA, possibility would have begun with
just a gentle walk with the other elephants.

Possibility can be difficult to recognize
because it can present itself
as something very small:
A seed that will grow if watered to become
a beautiful tree that produces continuous fruit.

Possibility may be an inner prompting that,
if allowed to travel to our intellect without obeying,
we will think away.
Perhaps possibility is a door, and intention the key
to open it with our *yes* being the strength to walk through.

Some doors require great sacrifice or loss as entry,
but if we surrender to their request we find that
the greatest possibility unfolds to become even more
than we could have imagined.
Such is the mystery and wonder of life.

May we always enter
fearlessly!

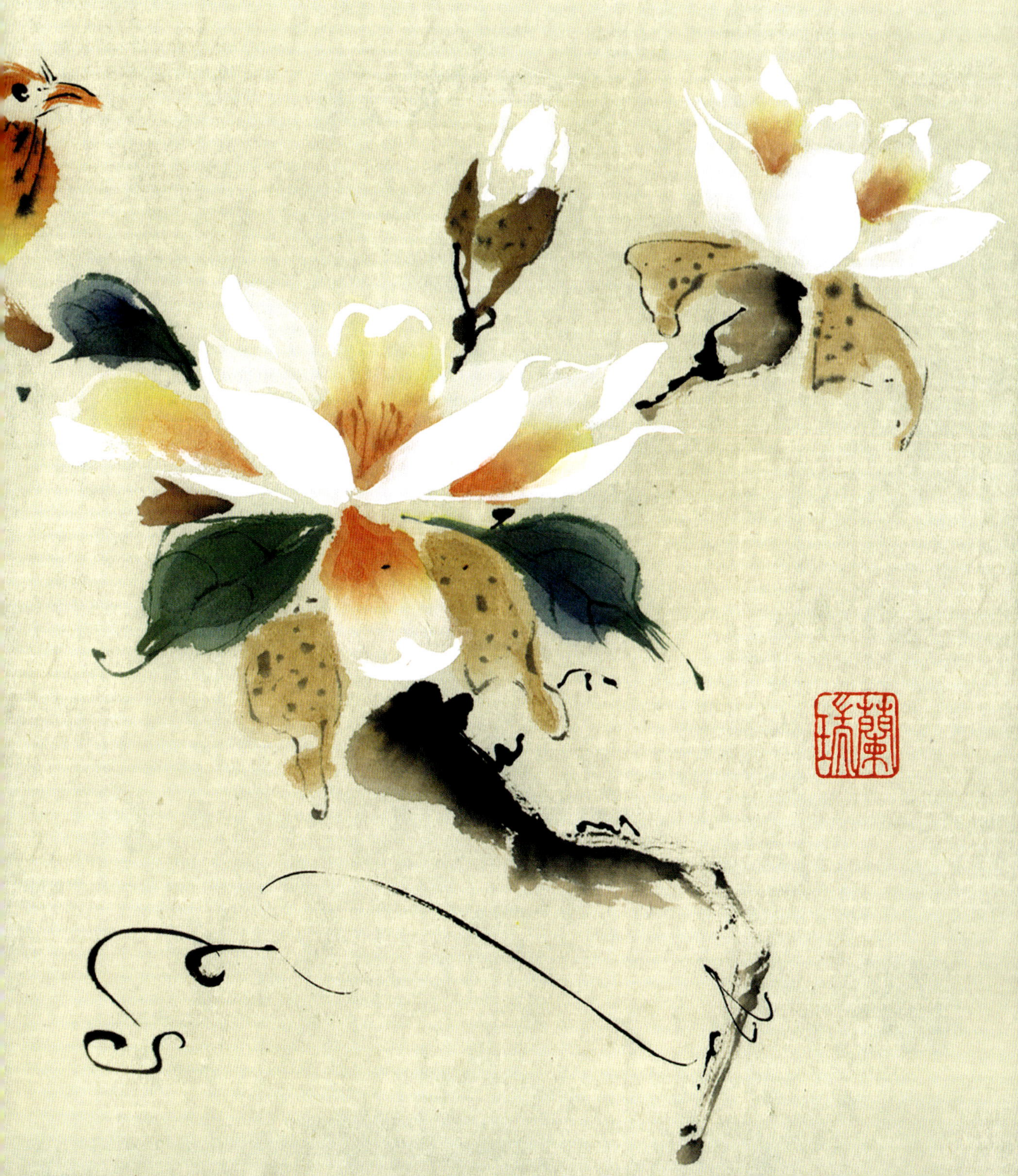

I've found being *happy / joyful*

is a *commitment*,

a *decision* that must be made regardless of my circumstances.

If I don't *surrender* to what appears to be insurmountable,

then enormous effort is needed to feel at *peace* again.

I choose joy.

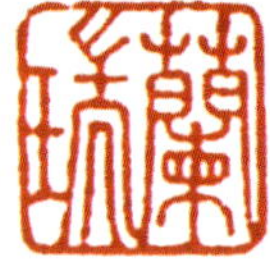

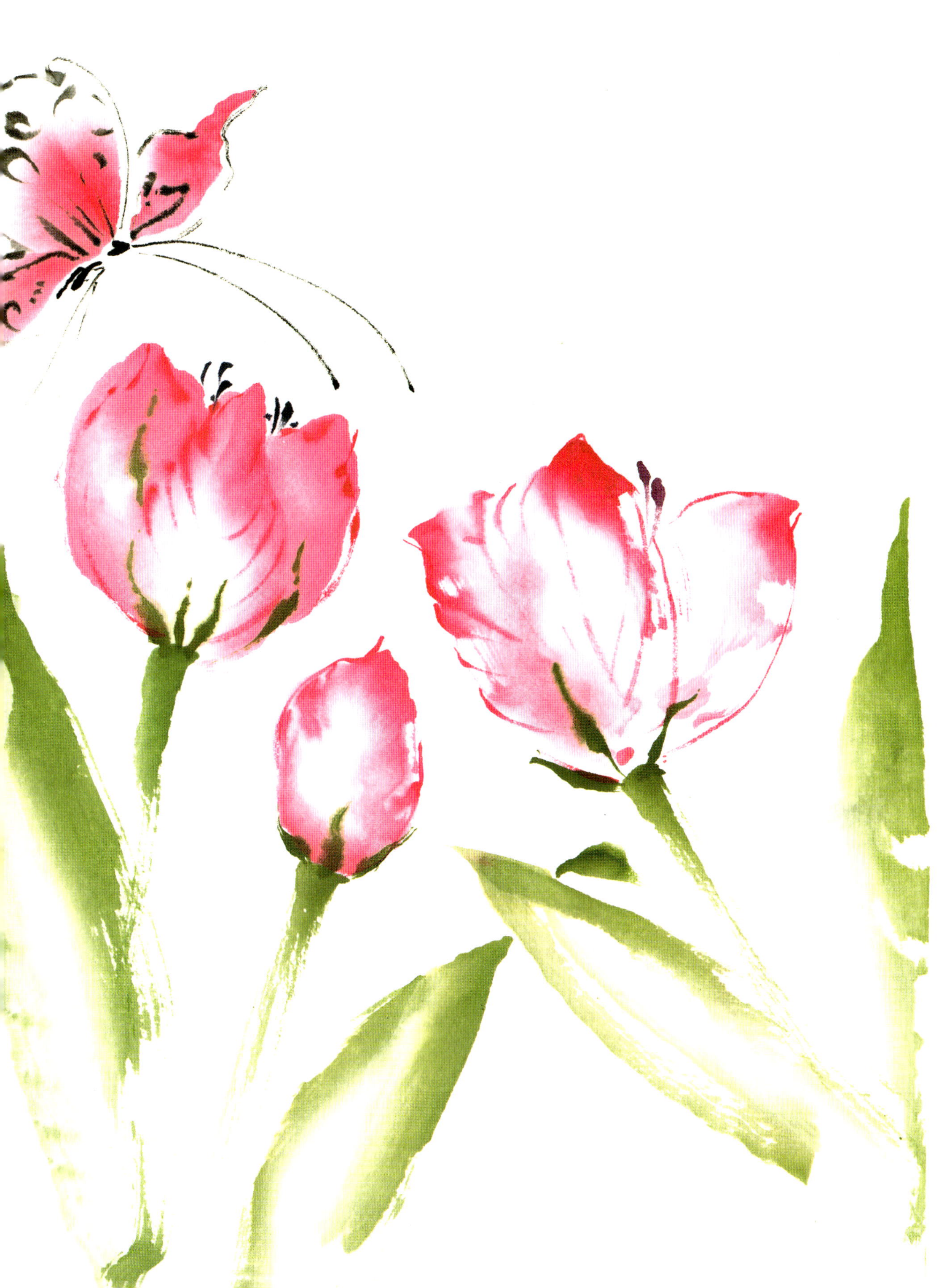

MEDITATION ON
Humor

Nietzsche and Freud both said, "Life is hard to bear."
Considering this, perhaps the greatest gift of all to have
as we journey through life is humor.
With humor we enter into our commonality and face our mortality.

Humor relaxes us.
Humor gives us hope.
Humor sees possibilities.
Humor helps us reframe the way we see.
Humor can help us survive a difficult day.
Humor tells us that no matter the circumstances, we will be O.K.

It surprised me to learn that both Martin Luther
and Abraham Lincoln,
two very heavy souls, employed humor in times of great stress.
Perhaps this allowed them to see more clearly
and to know that nothing,
as horrific as it may appear, is ever the final answer.
Perhaps we could resolve to take life just a bit less seriously
and perhaps this will allow greater joy in our lives.
Most importantly, humor helps us live life with Grace.

*May we live in the unforced
rhythms of Grace.*

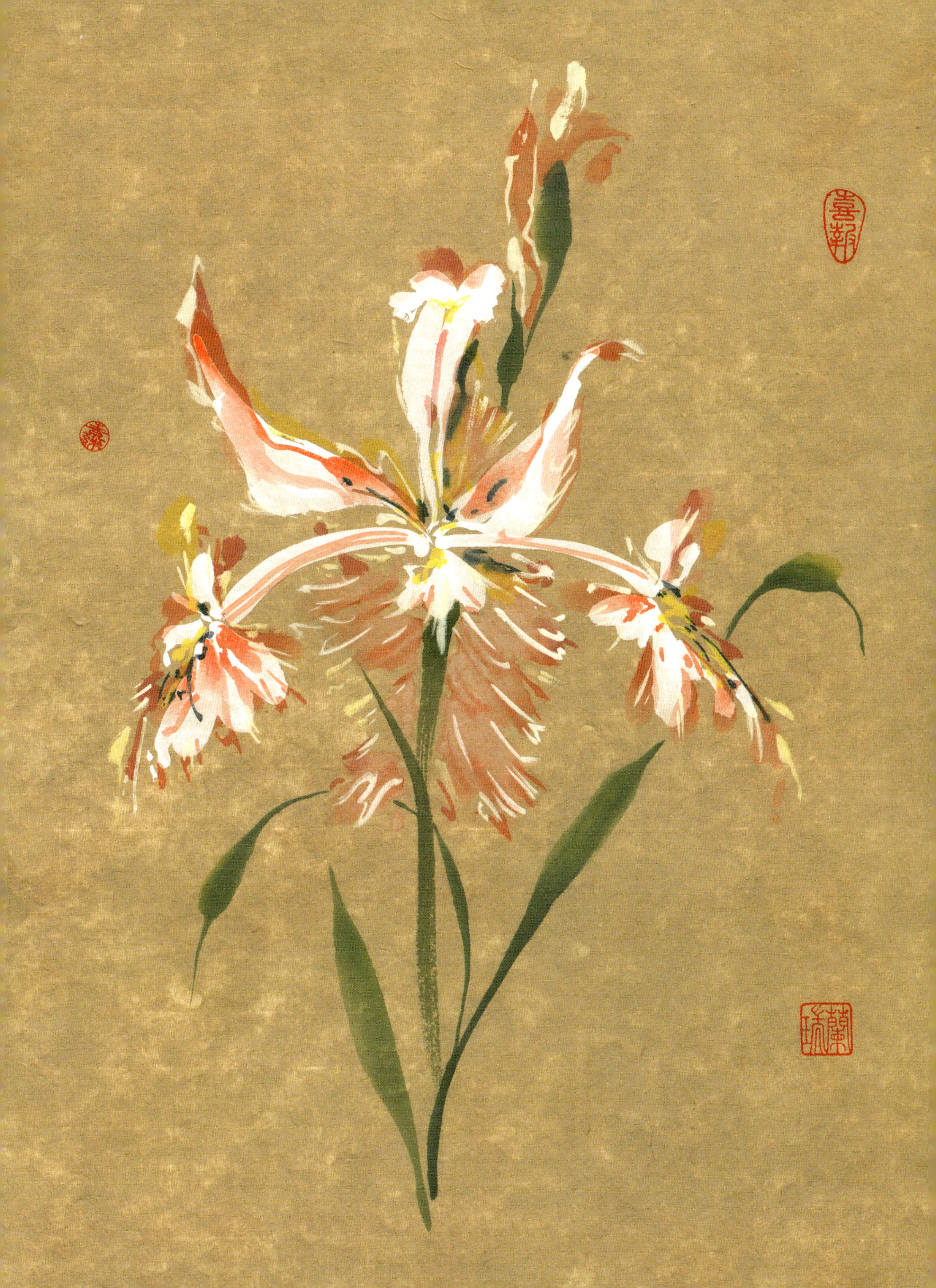

There is a hardening of the soul/spirit that
slowly creeps in each day,
rather like the incoming tide.
Knowing this to be true,
I set aside time each morning to make the
world I inhabit new and fresh again.

Gratitude

becomes my vehicle for this transformation.

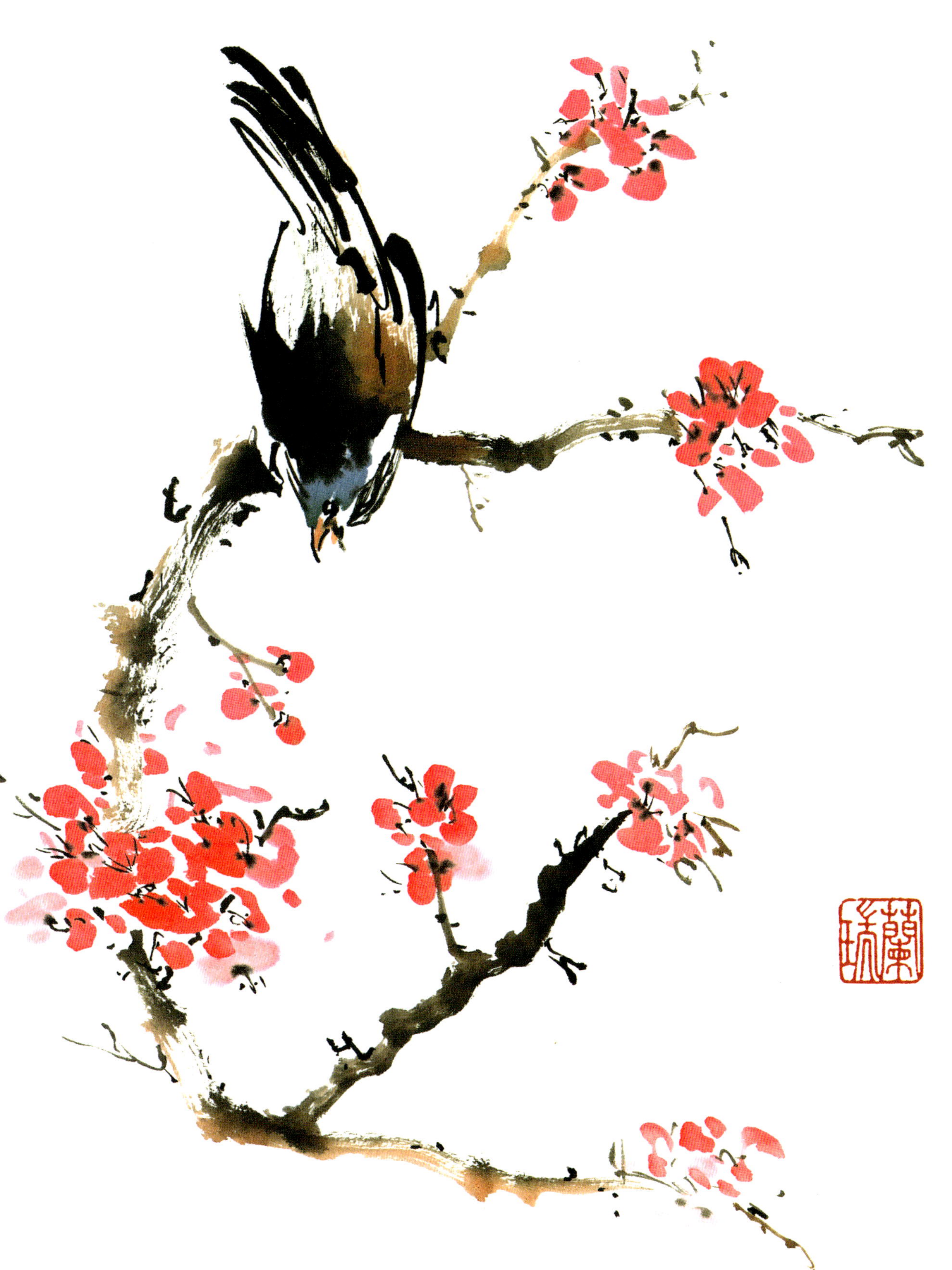

Have you ever wondered why so many things we worry about never come to pass?

Life is unpredictable so why not resist concern about a future that is always opaque?

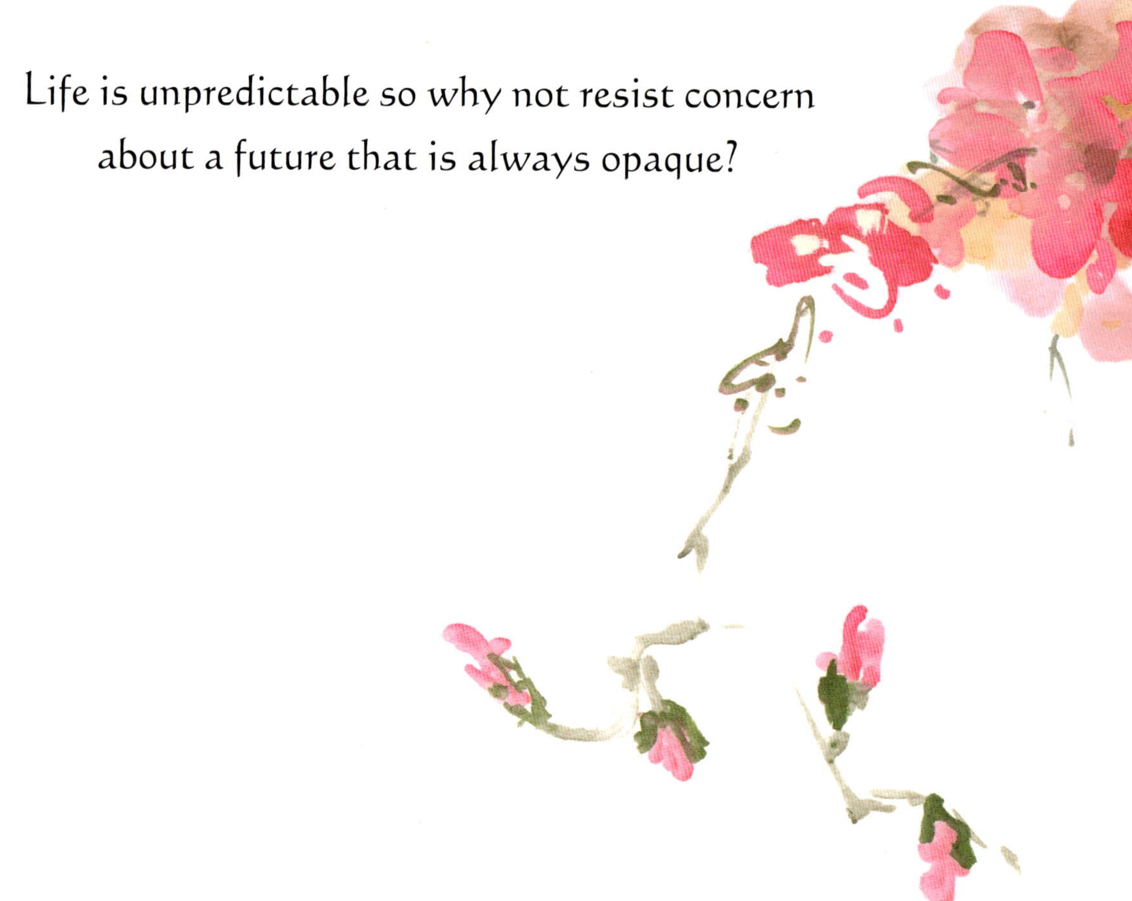

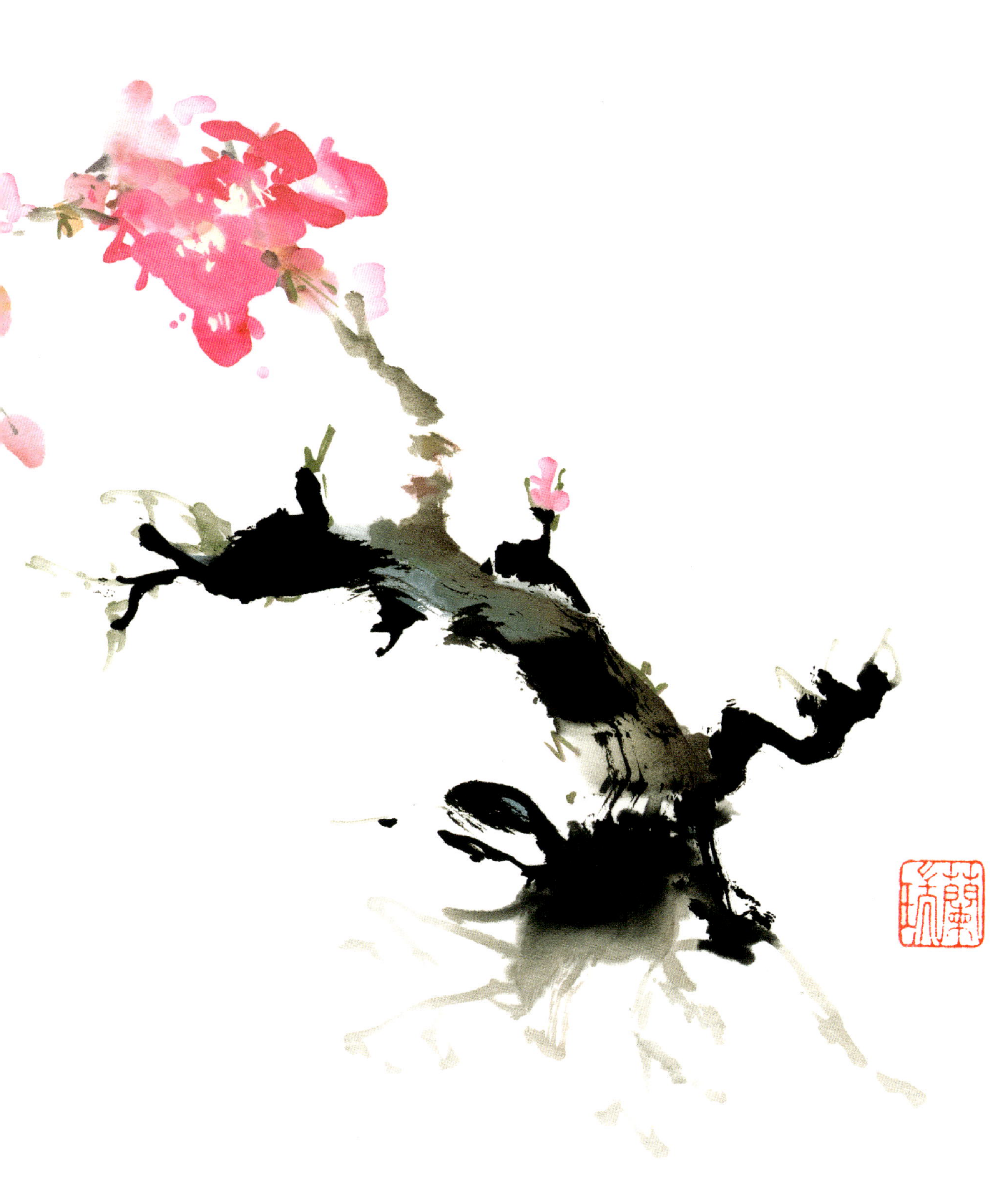

Each day we're confronted with a decision.
Will I react to my circumstances or
make that decision to be

grateful?

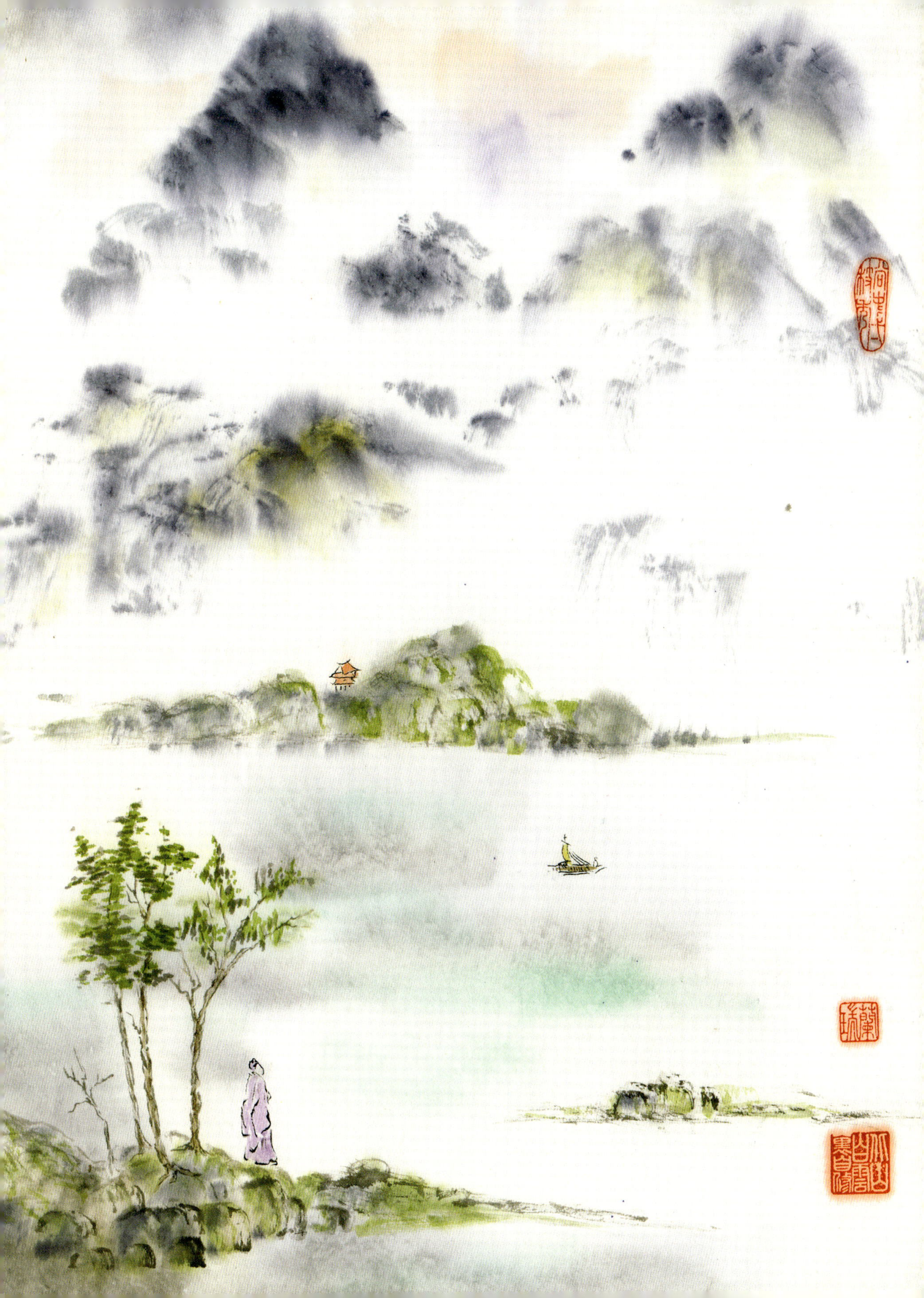

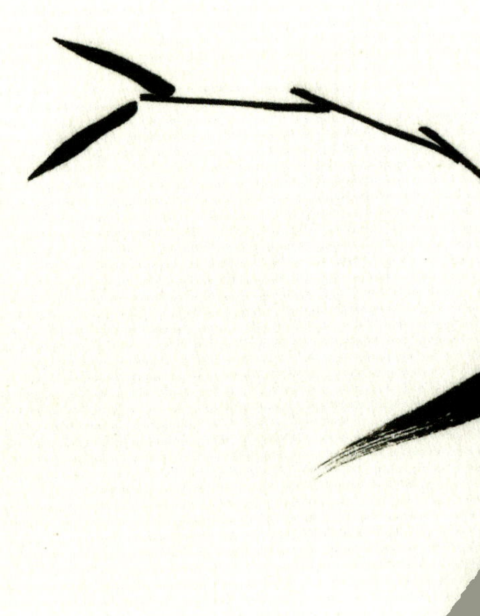

Will I be fully present in the moment, not fearful of the future or dwelling on the past?

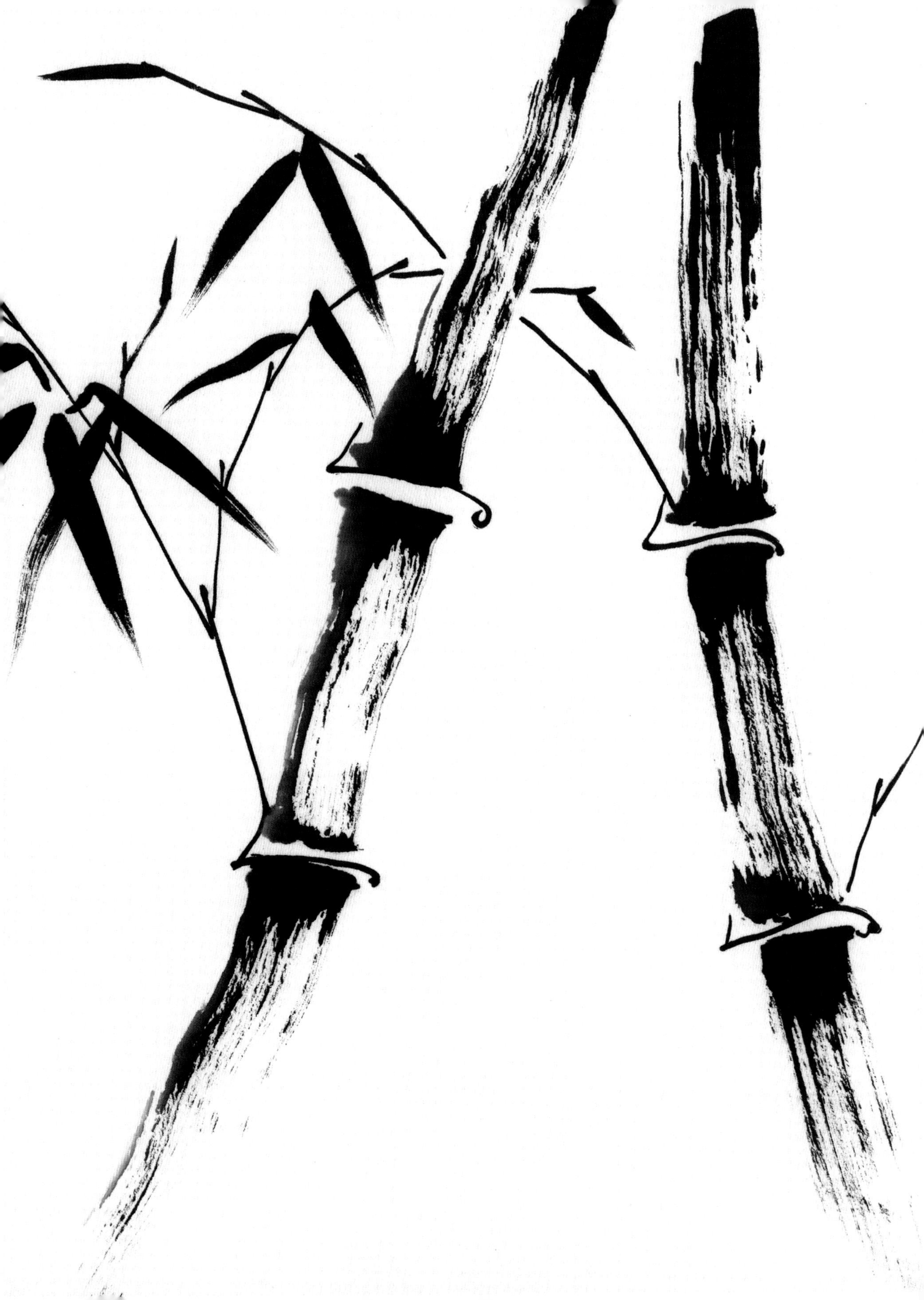

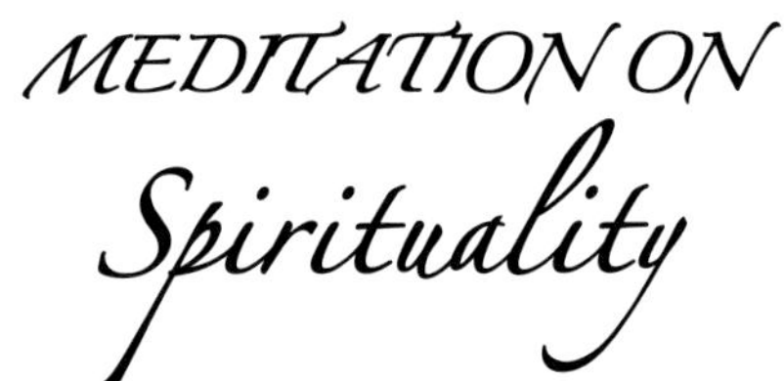

How do we go forward bringing spirituality into every aspect of our everyday lives?

It's probably safe to say that most people with a religious or spiritual nature agree that there's a force called a higher power or God that created the universe and our world.

Taking that further, this Creator made man in His image that is like Himself and gave man authority over all living things.

The next thing He gave man was unconditional free will, with the admonition that if man did well...no problem...but if not, then sin/hardship/trouble was waiting at the door for him.

Throughout history we see man doing some very good things and some very bad things. When disaster strikes, man asks, "Why didn't God do something?"

He can't.

Bishop Desmond Tutu said, "For whatever reason, since humankind showed up on the scene, God does nothing without a human partner."

God needs a willing partner to actively mediate His reign of love and care in the world.

Man is the only sentient being with this free will.
All other creatures do as they are told.
If you don't believe this... just watch a nesting dove.

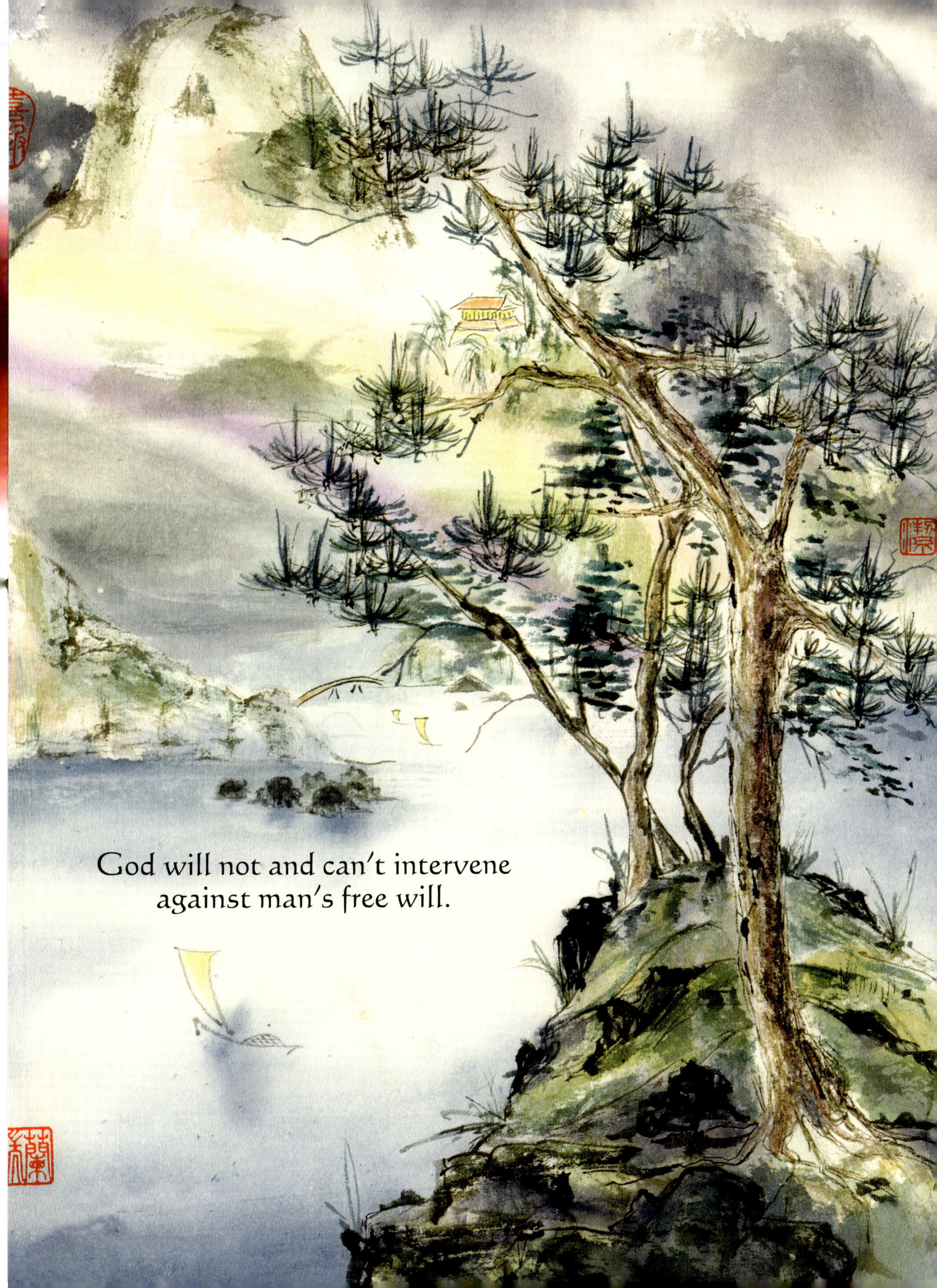

God will not and can't intervene
against man's free will.

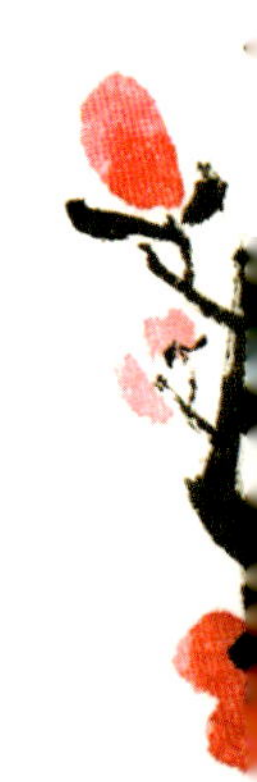

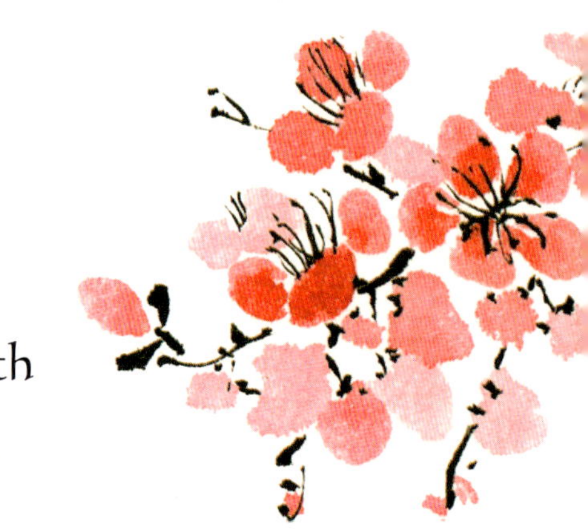

Please take a deep breath
and really consider....

This is a moment in time that will never come again...
treasure it.

An awesome truth spoken to me and my fellow artists
as we journeyed through Japan.

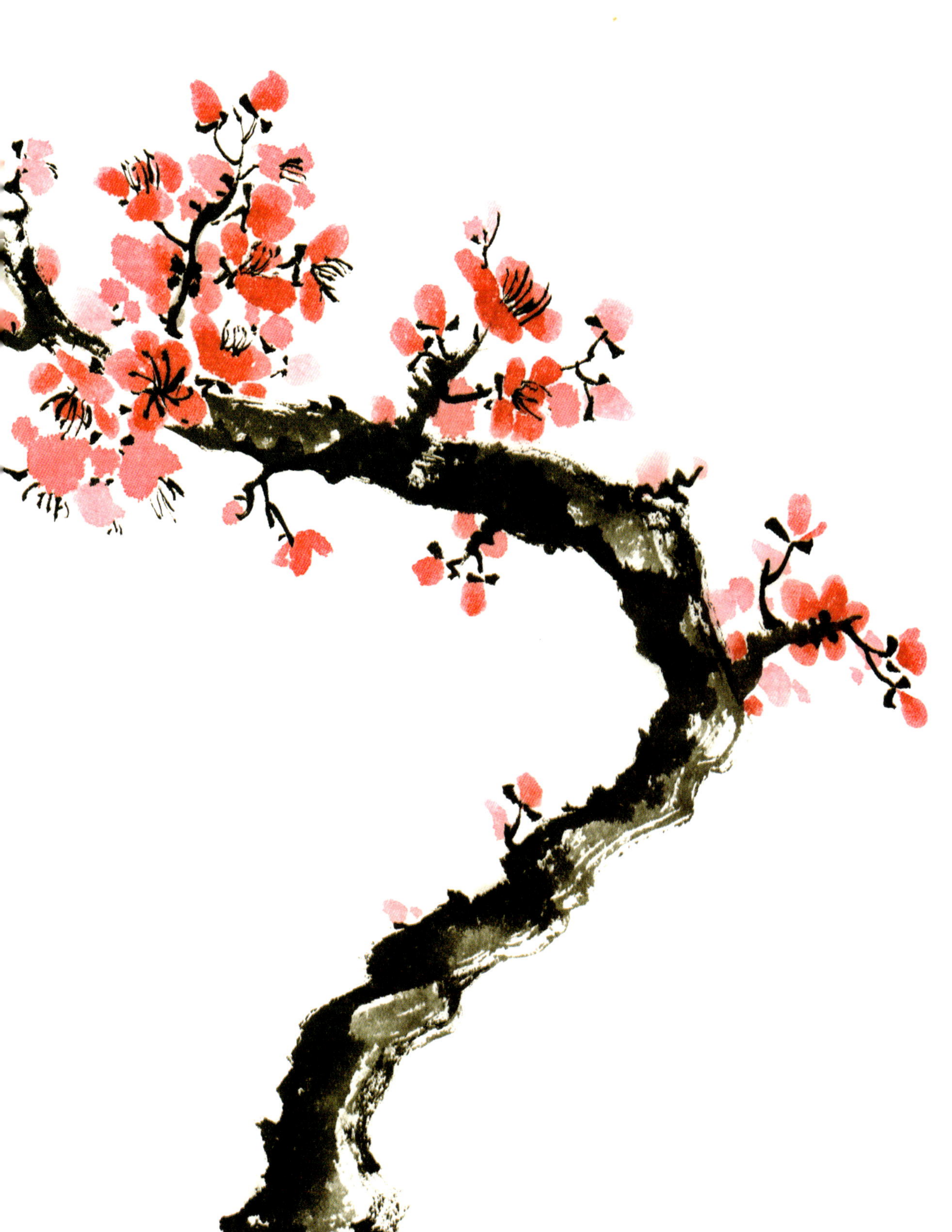

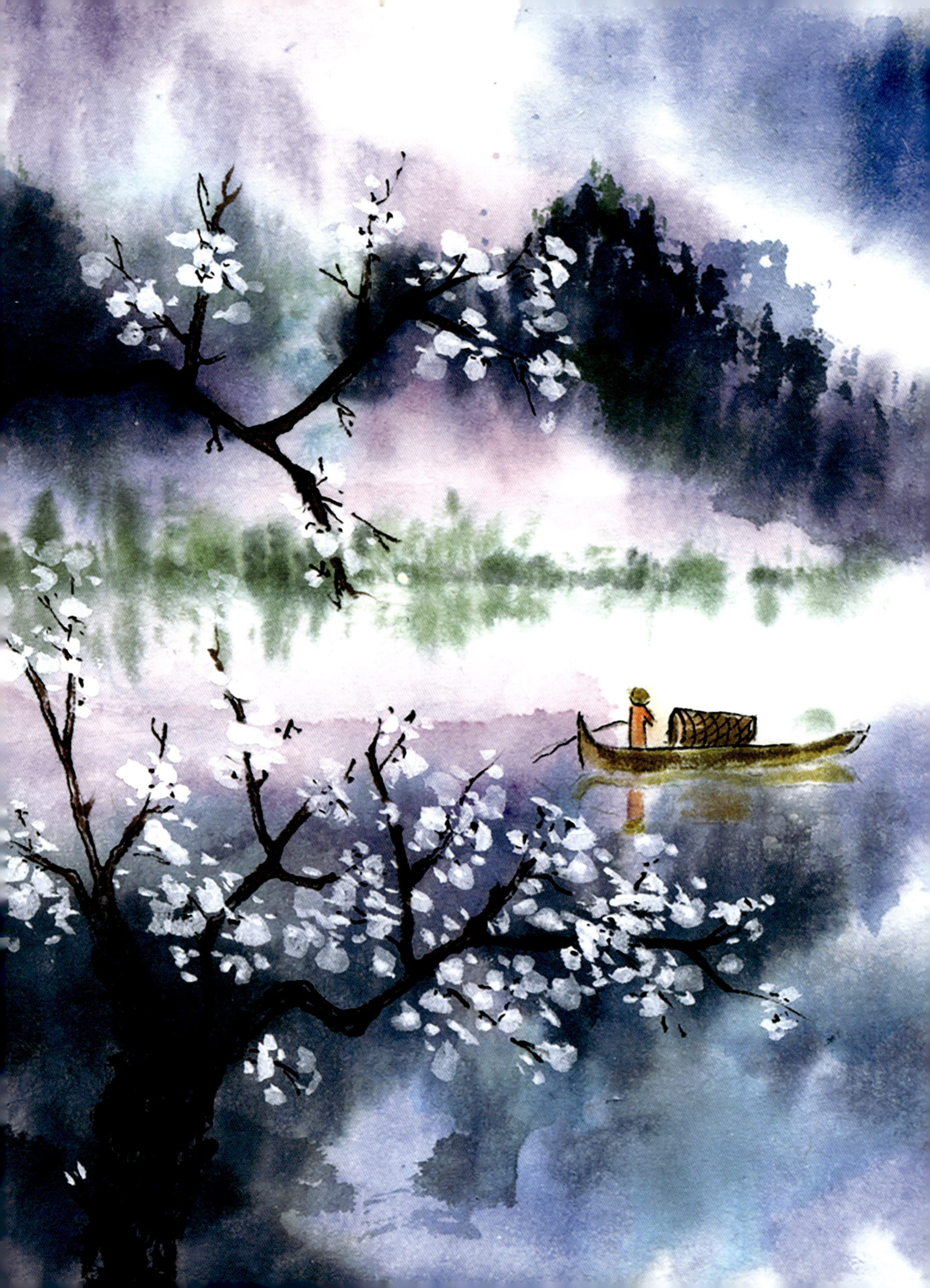

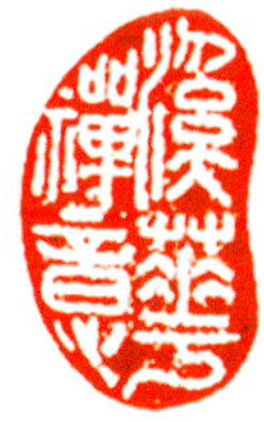

We're all praying for God to intervene...
perhaps God is waiting for us as He will not intervene
against our free will.

If we're fully present in each moment, grateful for all that is,
we open the door to love and are touched by Grace.

May we all abide in the
unforced rhythms of Grace.

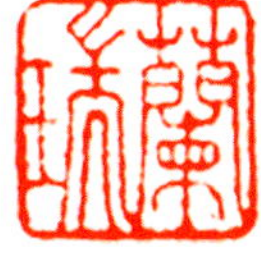

MEDITATION ON Healing

One of the greatest gifts man has been given is the ability to laugh, and there are now scientific studies backing up the theory that laughter can not only heal us but keep us well.

If we step back and look at laughter, it's quite a strange gift, but its purpose becomes clearer with the strange alchemy that happens when we realize that humor in the face of a difficult situation diffuses it and somehow gives us hope. This hope produces faith…faith in a better day tomorrow. Humor then can even become a weapon that is used against anxiety, fear and defeat.

What I would like us to seriously think about is, can we surrender to the notion that there really is not much we can control and in fighting that fact we refuse to surrender to the humor in any given situation. Great comics usually discuss really dreadful situations and make us laugh about them. Think about all the mother-in-law jokes.

As we re-enter the world we'll have many opportunities to be stressed out… just driving on the freeway will do it for starters. When we encounter a difficult situation, perhaps instead of responding in kind we could step back, take a deep breath and say isn't that interesting, and just let it slide. Seeing the humor in life's sometimes harrowing situations will do more to keep us healthy than anything we could do, and that's been scientifically proven.
May I leave you with some thoughts on humor by minds much wiser than mine…

Immanuel Kant said, "Laughter produces a feeling of health."
Sir William Osler regarded laughter as the "music of life."

Robert Burton in "Anatomy of Melancholy" said, "Humor makes the body young."

Hobbes said, "Laughter is a passion of sudden glory."

Fyodor Dostoyevsky wrote in "The Adolescent,"
"If you wish to glimpse inside a human soul and get to know a man…
if he laughs well, he's a good man."

And finally, the Bible tells us "a merry heart works like a medicine."

May we all strive for a

merry heart.

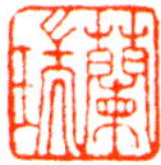

How strange that the simple act of just *smiling* can give us a *happy heart.*

Try it!

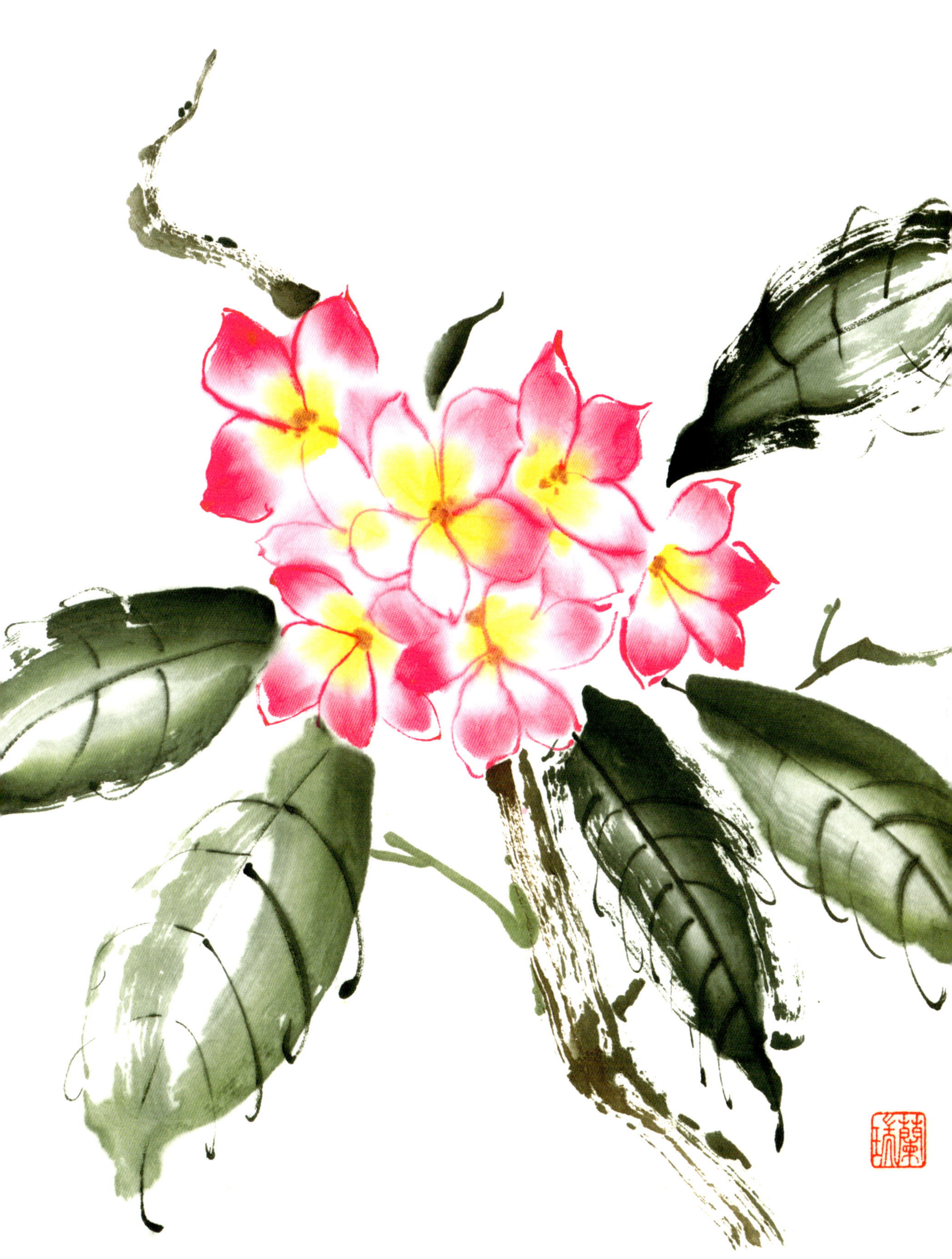

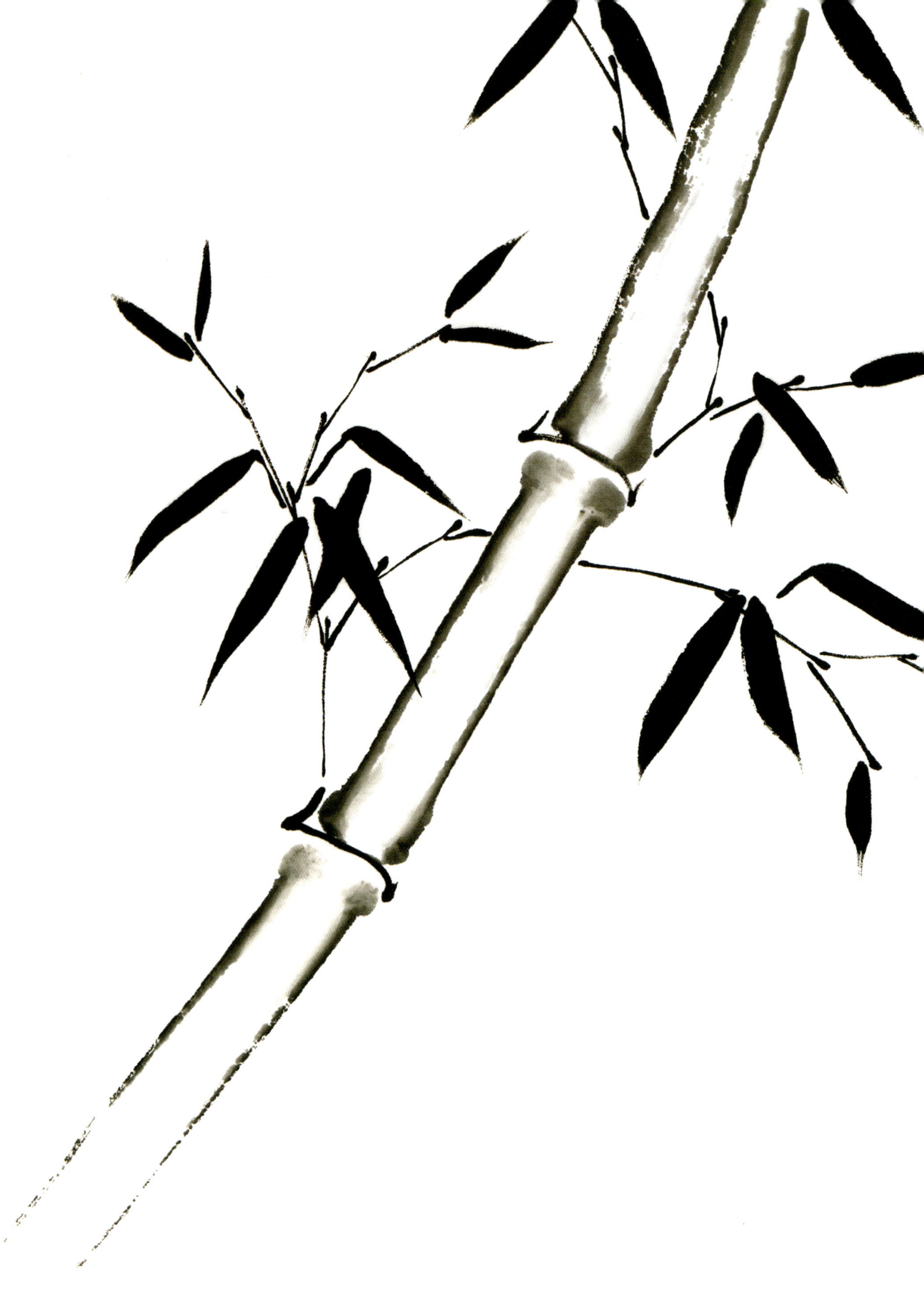

The mystery in life is that we can decide to place ourselves as observers of our lives, letting irritants, anxieties and concerns drift past us as we release them.

MEDITATION ON Understanding

It's amazing how understanding brings clarity to all of our meditations. Without understanding it's impossible to have stability as we will be tossed about by every idea that comes our way, unable to judge the good from the bad. With a firm foundation, being grounded, always seeking understanding, we know that all is well, even when we might think otherwise.

Without understanding spiritual growth is impossible. Of all the things he could ask for, King Solomon asked God for wisdom knowing he needed great understanding if he was to judge and lead his people. If we seek wisdom, being able to look deep into our inner man, we can correct course if necessary.

Without understanding how can we see possibilities and determine which course is best for us to take? Would we even begin to understand opportunities? Life would be opaque to us and we'd be unable to even begin a new path. May truth break through to us, opening our eyes to a possibility we might have completely missed.

Without understanding I'm afraid we'd be humorless, not understanding the irony, the humor in many if not most situations. If we don't take everything so seriously, then we won't overreact and use a cannon instead of a slingshot.

I wonder if we can be kind without understanding. Understanding requires us to look past the superficial, what we think we see with our eyes or hear with our ears and look instead to what God would have us see and do. May we be completely non-judgmental and kind towards our fellow man.

Without understanding we could not live in harmony. We would be responding to what we think we hear and see without having discernment and listening with our heart. With understanding we will keep no record of wrongs and always be yielding, never insisting that our way is the right way.

Without understanding we could never love. We would always be finding fault, reacting from our own narrow perspective, fearful and doubting of everyone and everything. In defining love, the Apostle Paul said that love is not self-seeking. May we seek to understand what we're hearing and then learn to be like the Bamboo and bend, conceding that there could just possibly be some truth that we were missing and always allow another opinion without feeling threatened.

Without understanding we would never be still enough to listen to our bodies when they are in need of attention and possibly repair and bring healing to them. May we always be able to understand the true heart of every matter for our health's sake.

Most importantly, without understanding we wouldn't even begin to act like a spiritual being living in a rented tabernacle. It's been said of God that His thoughts are not our thoughts and His ways not ours. May we always seek understanding that we might discern the truth in every situation. When we can do that we are truly a spiritual being not acting on carnal intentions.

May our goal always be to seek out wisdom for then we will truly understand with our heart and be able to easily demonstrate these most worthy attributes.

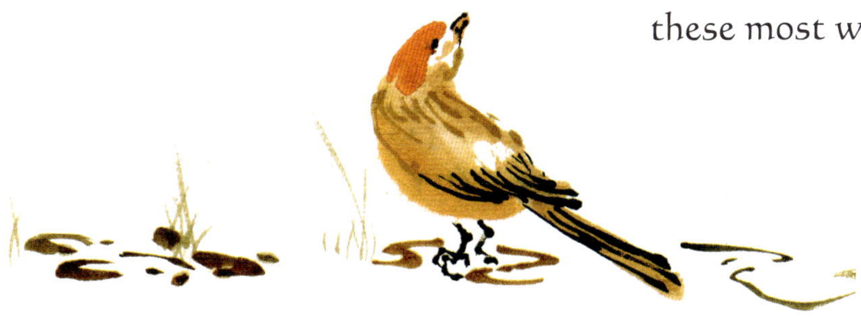

MEDITATION ON
Kindness

I never thought of being kind or if I was kind…
I had always assumed I was a kind person because
I was never deliberately unkind.

The stillness of the pandemic allowed me to pull back and reflect… it slowed me down enough to realize that wasn't enough. To be truly kind, I needed to be fully aware of my presence in the world in every encounter… no matter how small.

I needed to be fully present in each moment, each interaction, and ask what is required in this moment, what is my effect on the other person in this encounter. I started seeing how abrupt I could be in e-mails as I made a conscious effort to be kind and made my notes softer, less direct. I realized that I could be overbearing and insistent but only when I felt it was beneficial to the other person. It wouldn't be enough for me to think I was kind… did the person on the other end of the interaction think so or did they feel diminished, discounted?

I realized that being impatient is actually being unkind, and that being kind, showing kindness, requires work. One can't be thoughtless, assuming the other person knows you are a person of good will. The importance of civilities loomed large. Service people who are so easy to disregard... a waiter is not just someone there to serve me but rather an equal human soul with hopes, fears and dreams. Could I begin to see my connectedness with all of humanity? Would I be able to step further back, outside of myself to see how my actions are perceived?

This meditating on kindness and consciously practicing it for over a year led me to such a deep understanding that I put it in my book "WHAT IF…We Have the Power to Change Our Lives." Simply stated, I wrote:

"WHAT IF we make a conscious effort to be kind, no matter the circumstances… And WHAT IF that has such a positive outcome that we decide to make it a lifelong practice."

"WHAT IF we begin to understand that being kind is really being loving and…WHAT IF that discovery brings us so much love in return that we wouldn't think of turning back."

Finally, from Rumi, the Persian poet, "Your acts of kindness are iridescent wings of divine love, which linger and continue to uplift others long after your sharing."

Why do you continue to practice at 90?

"Because I think I'm making progress."

- Pablo Casals

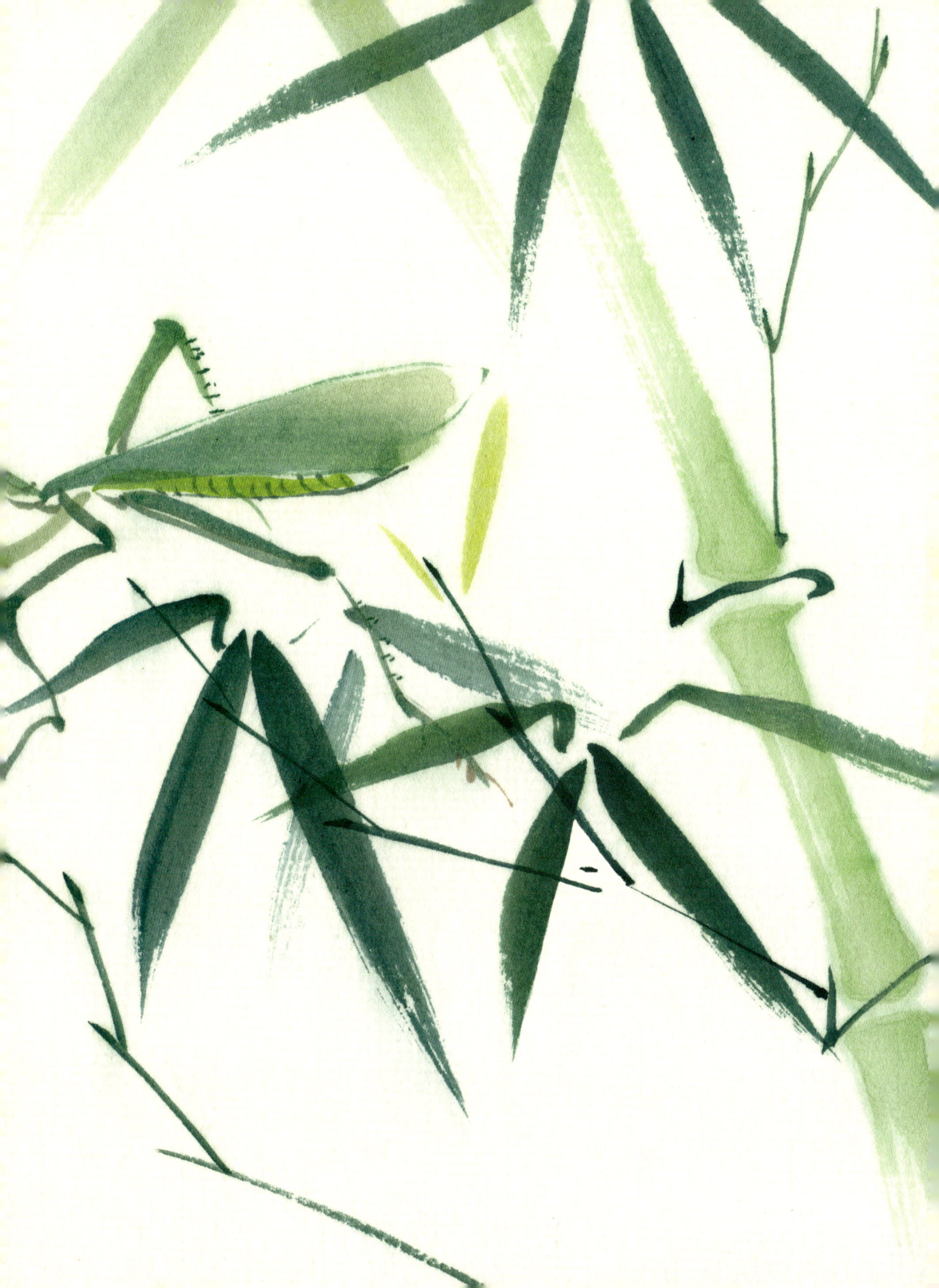

Thoughts On Loss:

I realized when we deeply feel the loss of a loved one what we're actually missing is a part of God that person contained, and the more truly human that person was, the more we long for the God in them.

In losing a great spirit having a human experience, perhaps the only remedy to healing is to open ourselves to contain even more of God's spirit. We then open to being comforted by the God of all comfort.

As Willie Nelson sang,

"It's not something you get over,
it's something you get through."

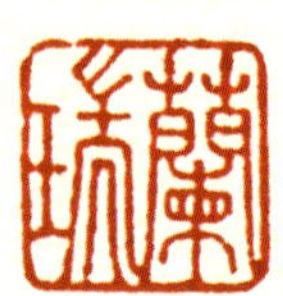

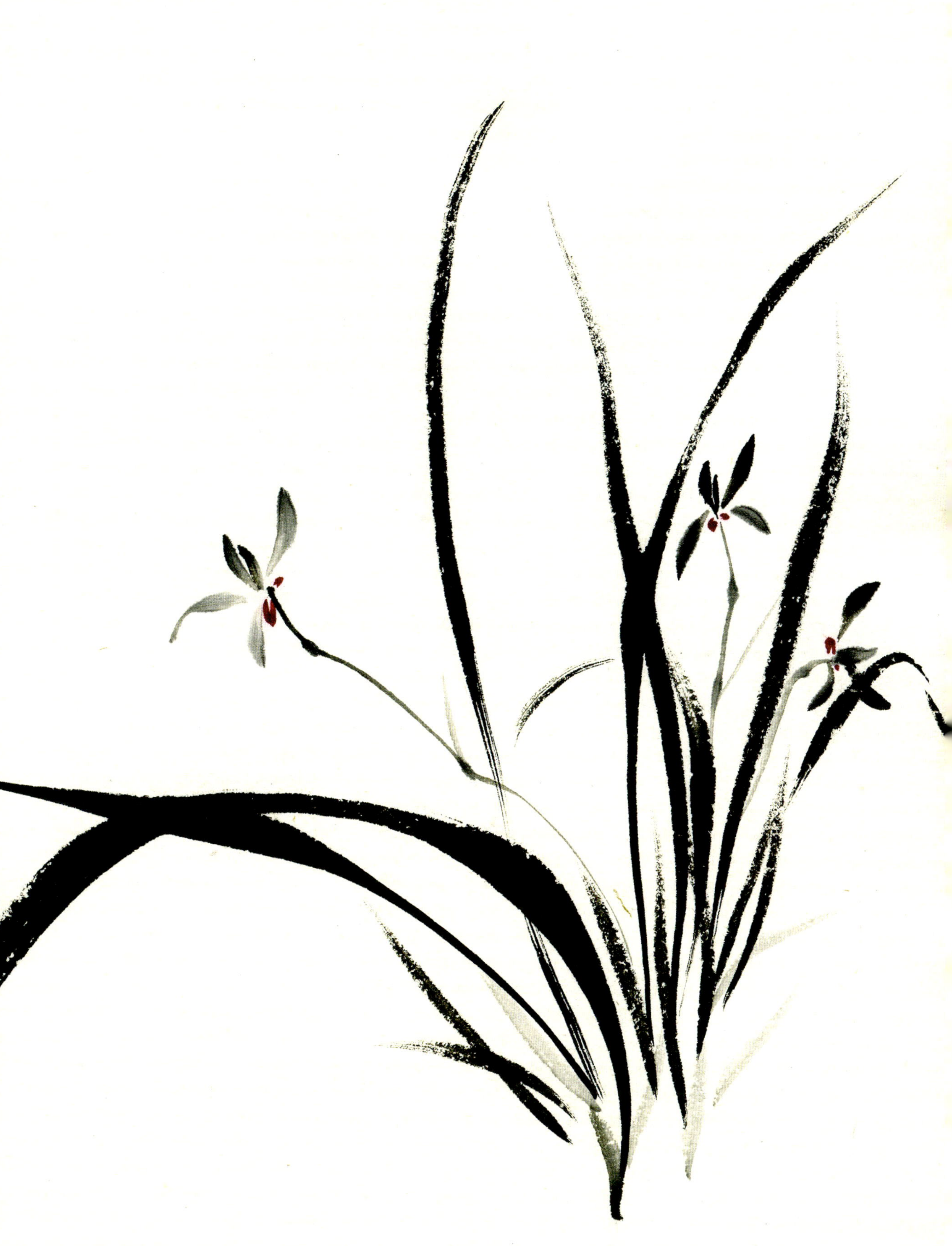

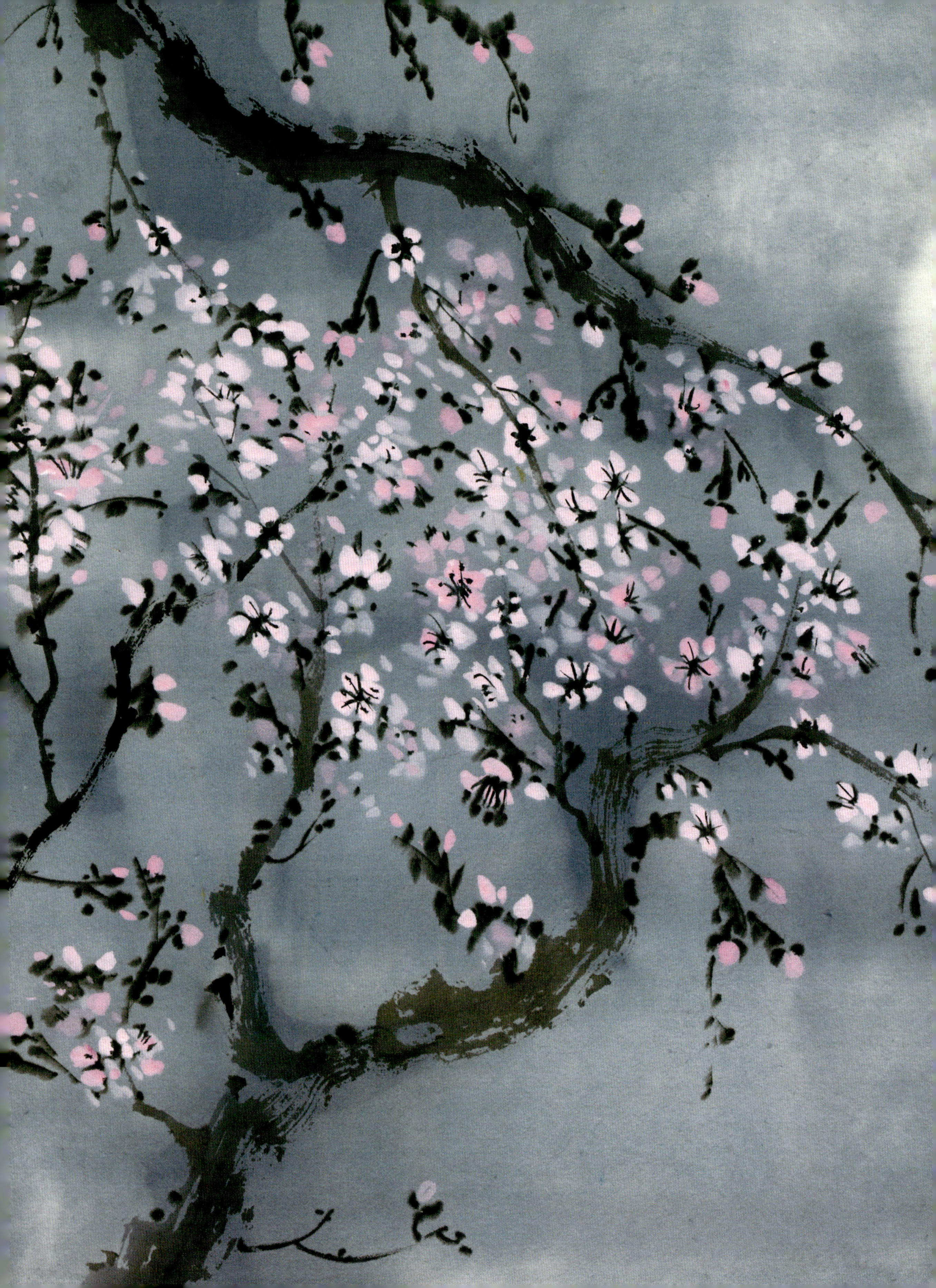

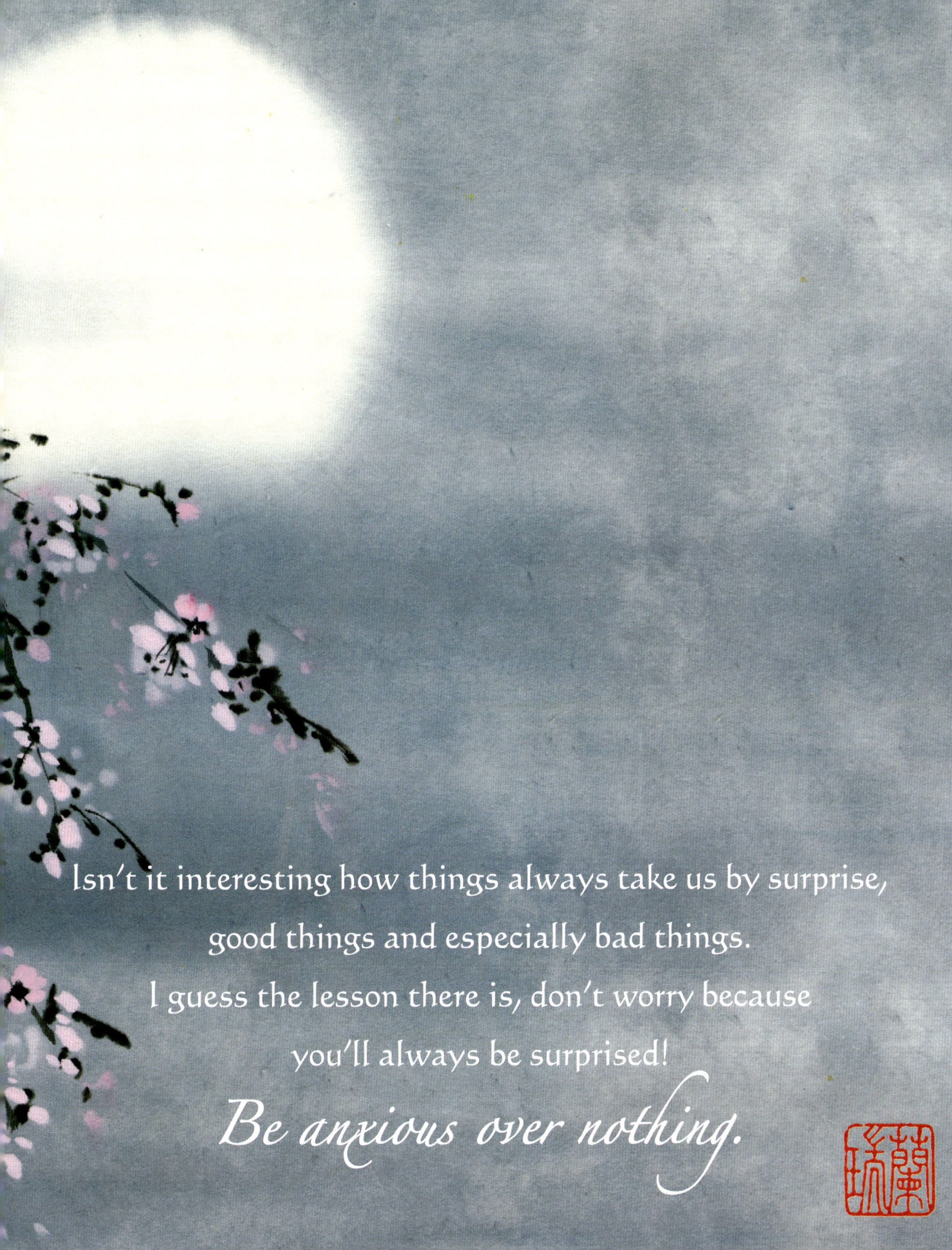

Isn't it interesting how things always take us by surprise, good things and especially bad things. I guess the lesson there is, don't worry because you'll always be surprised!

Be anxious over nothing.

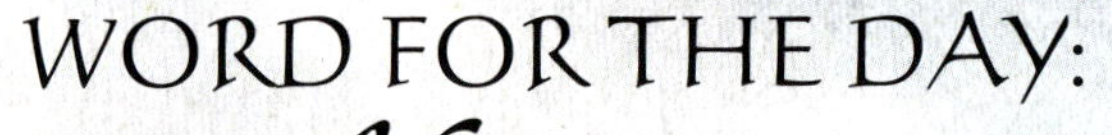

WORD FOR THE DAY:

"Bildungsroman,"

a literary genre that focuses on the psychological and moral growth of the protagonist from youth to adulthood in which character change is important.

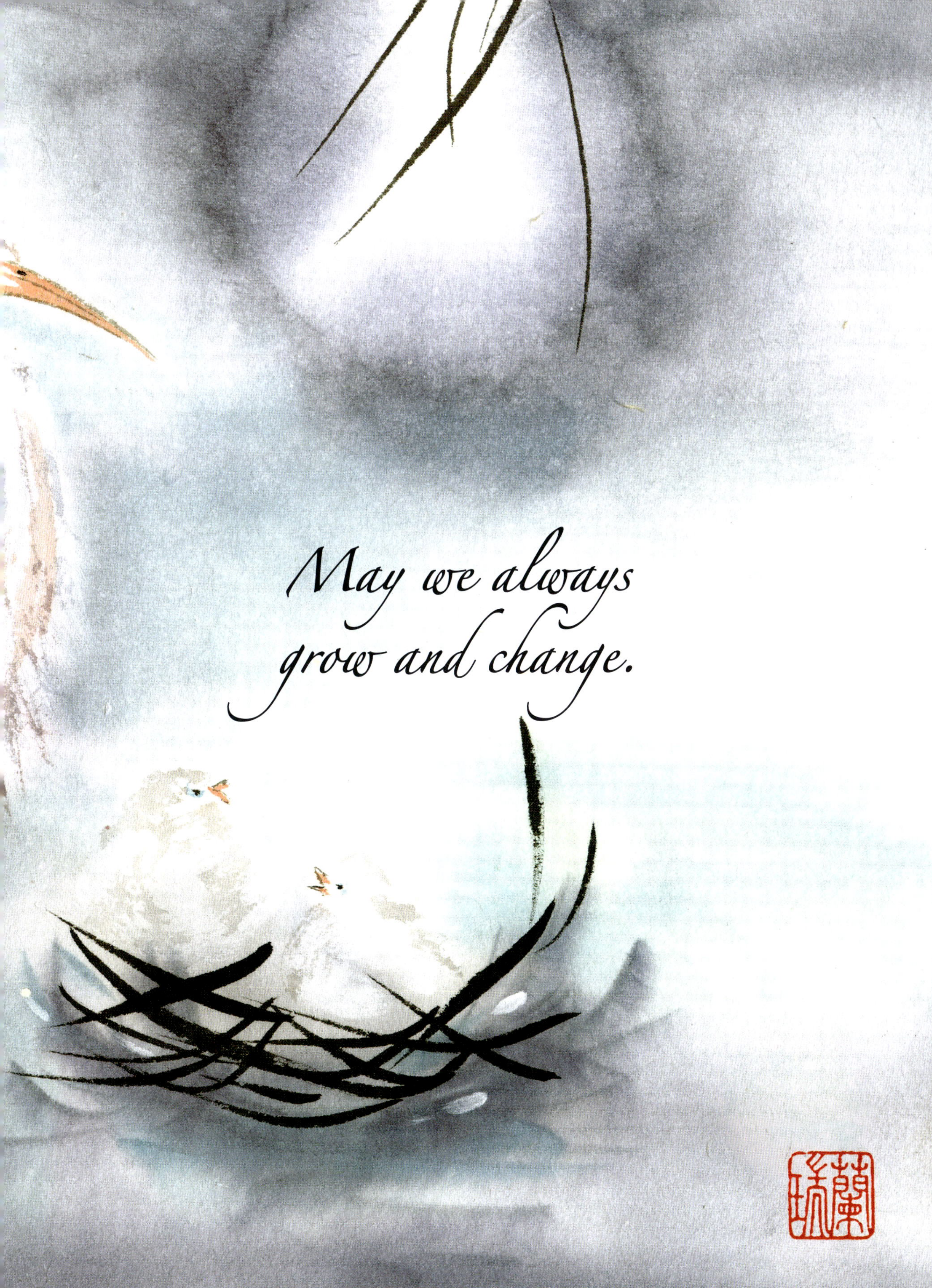
May we always grow and change.

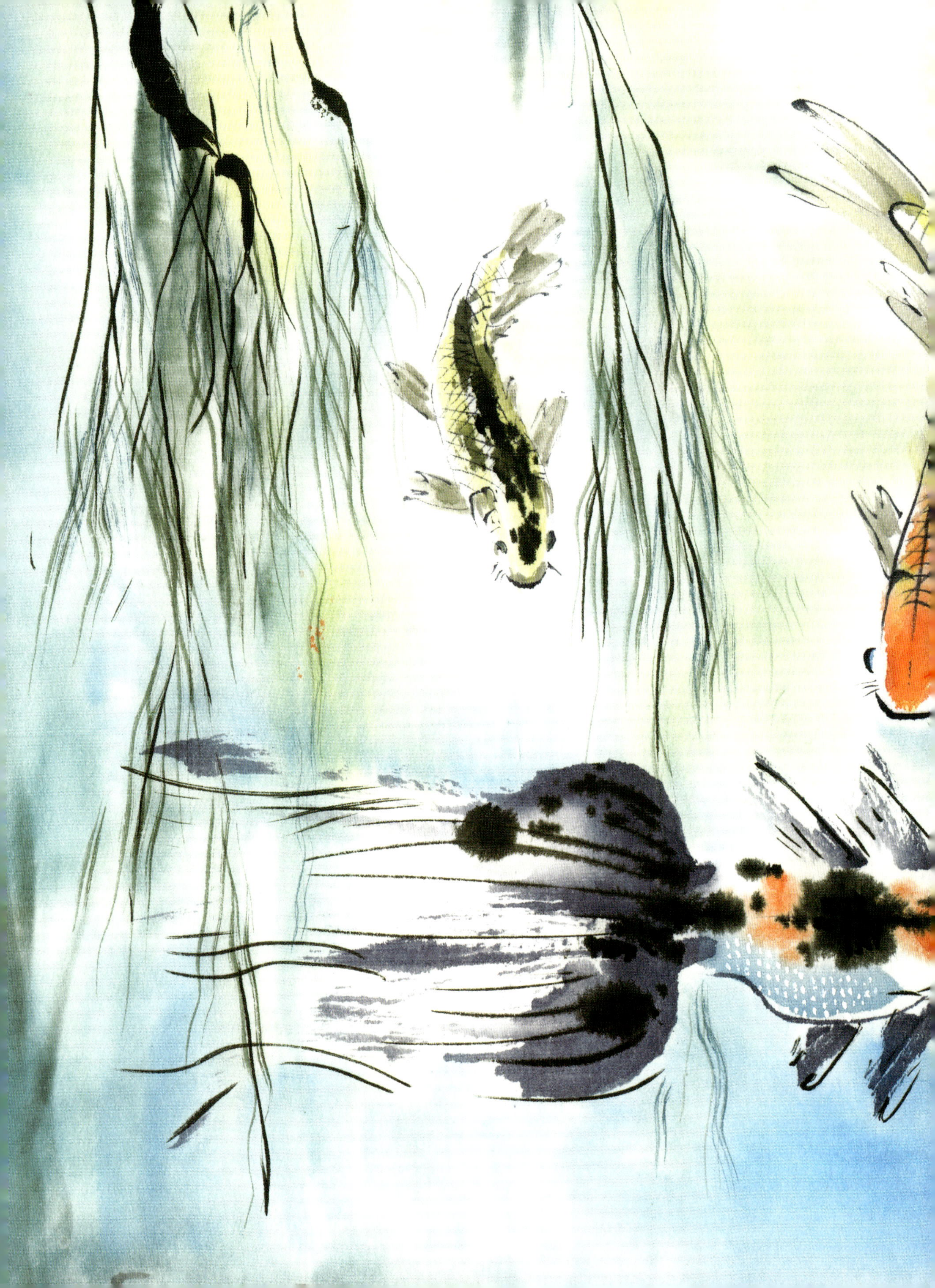

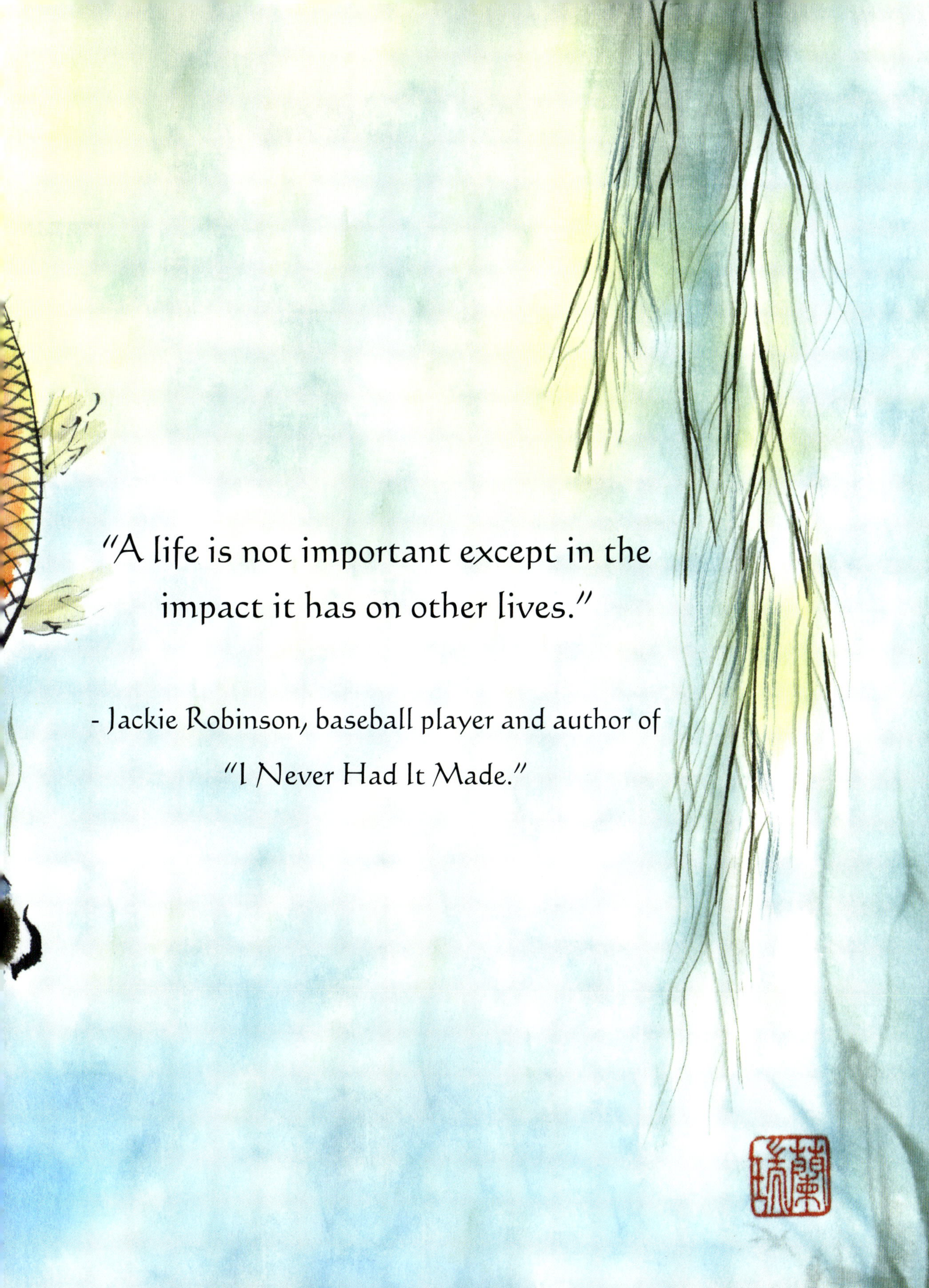

"A life is not important except in the impact it has on other lives."

- Jackie Robinson, baseball player and author of "I Never Had It Made."

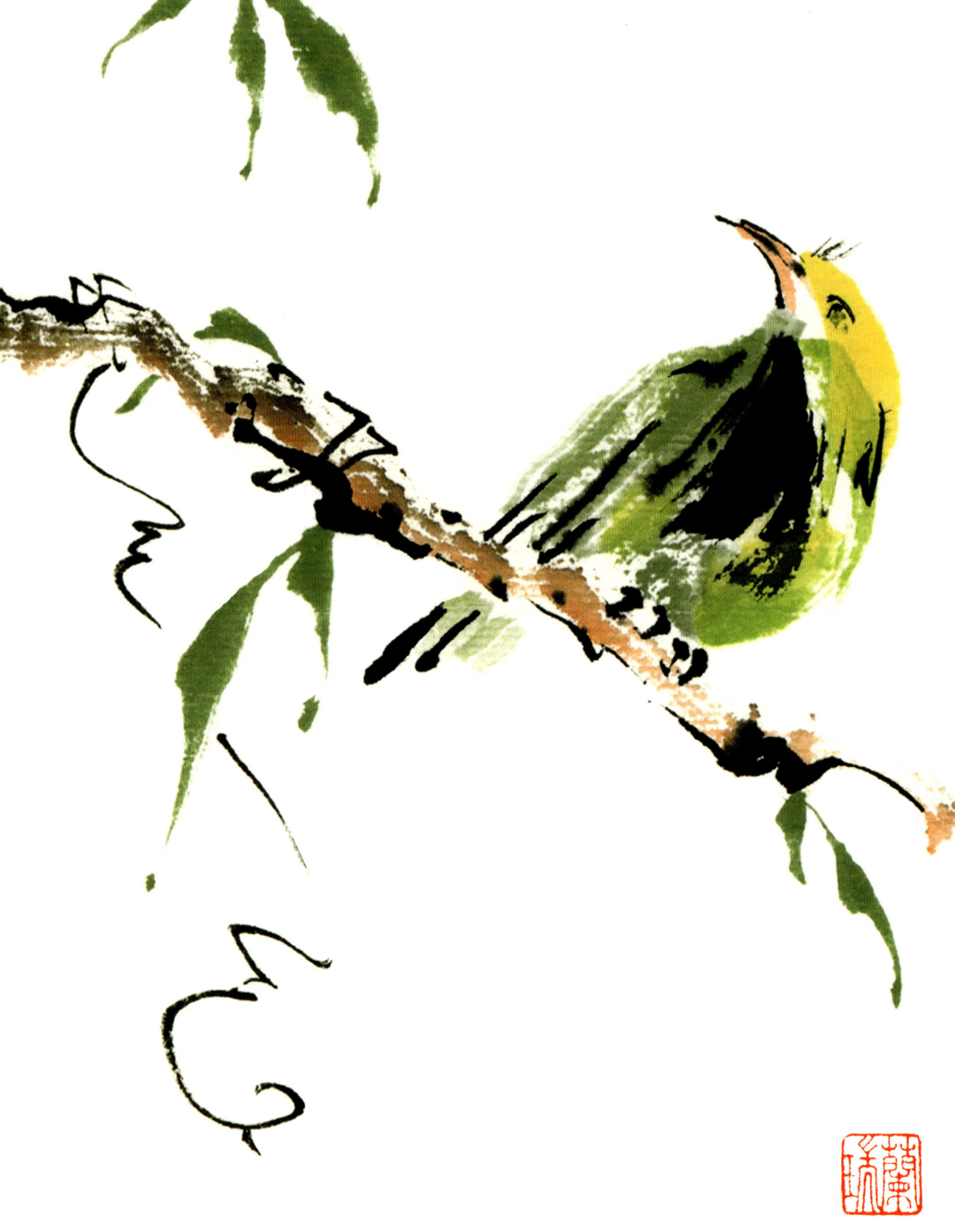

Ever notice how we fixate on the worst and
think about it constantly?
It's so much better to separate ourselves from our
thoughts and observe them, saying,
"I have a worried thought."

I always add to that…
"Isn't that interesting?"

We actually have ancient brains and irrational emotions that tend to take charge.
It's best to focus on problem-solving and not react emotionally.
Still your mind because an unmanaged brain will livestream worries nonstop.

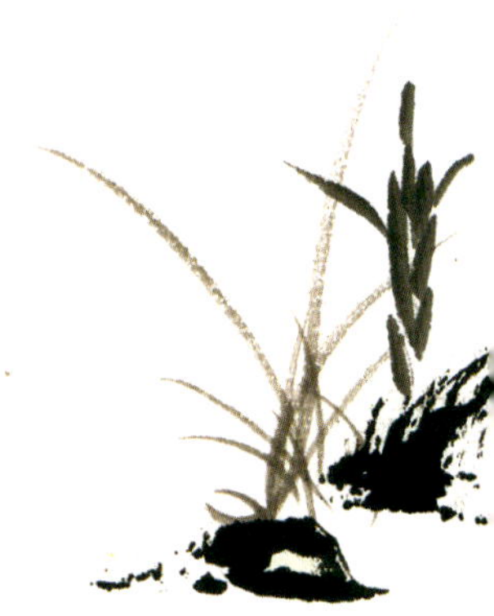

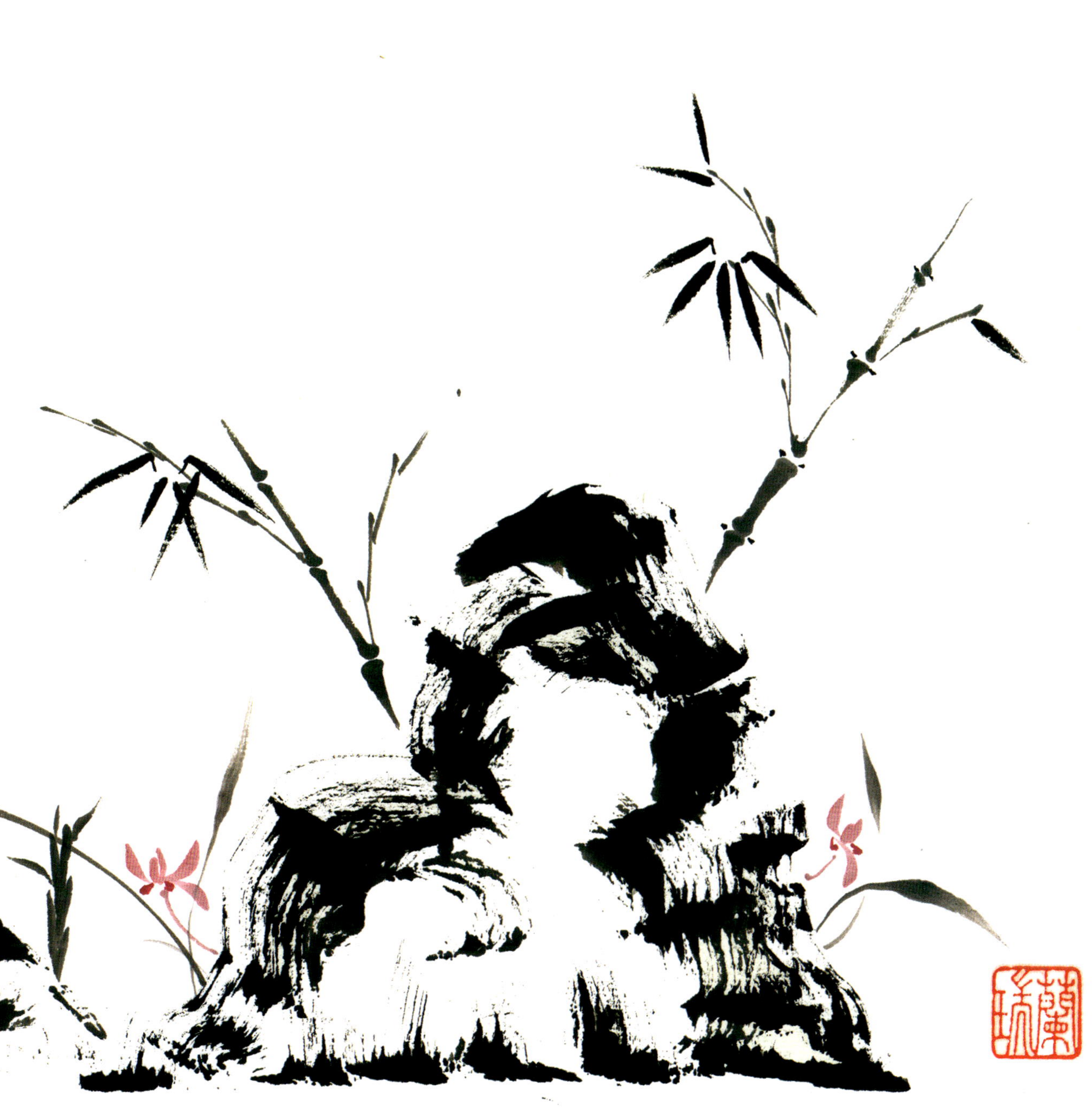

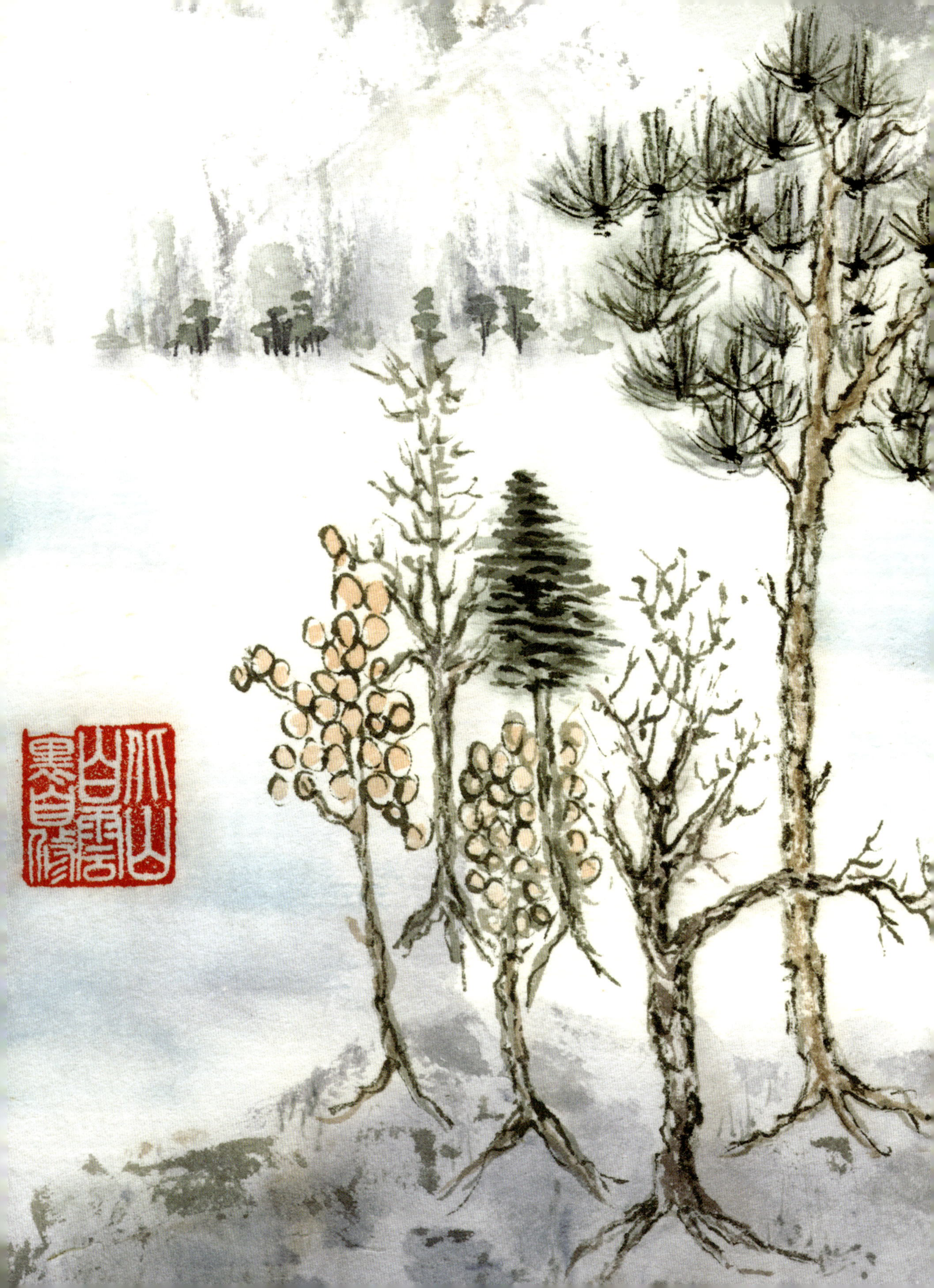

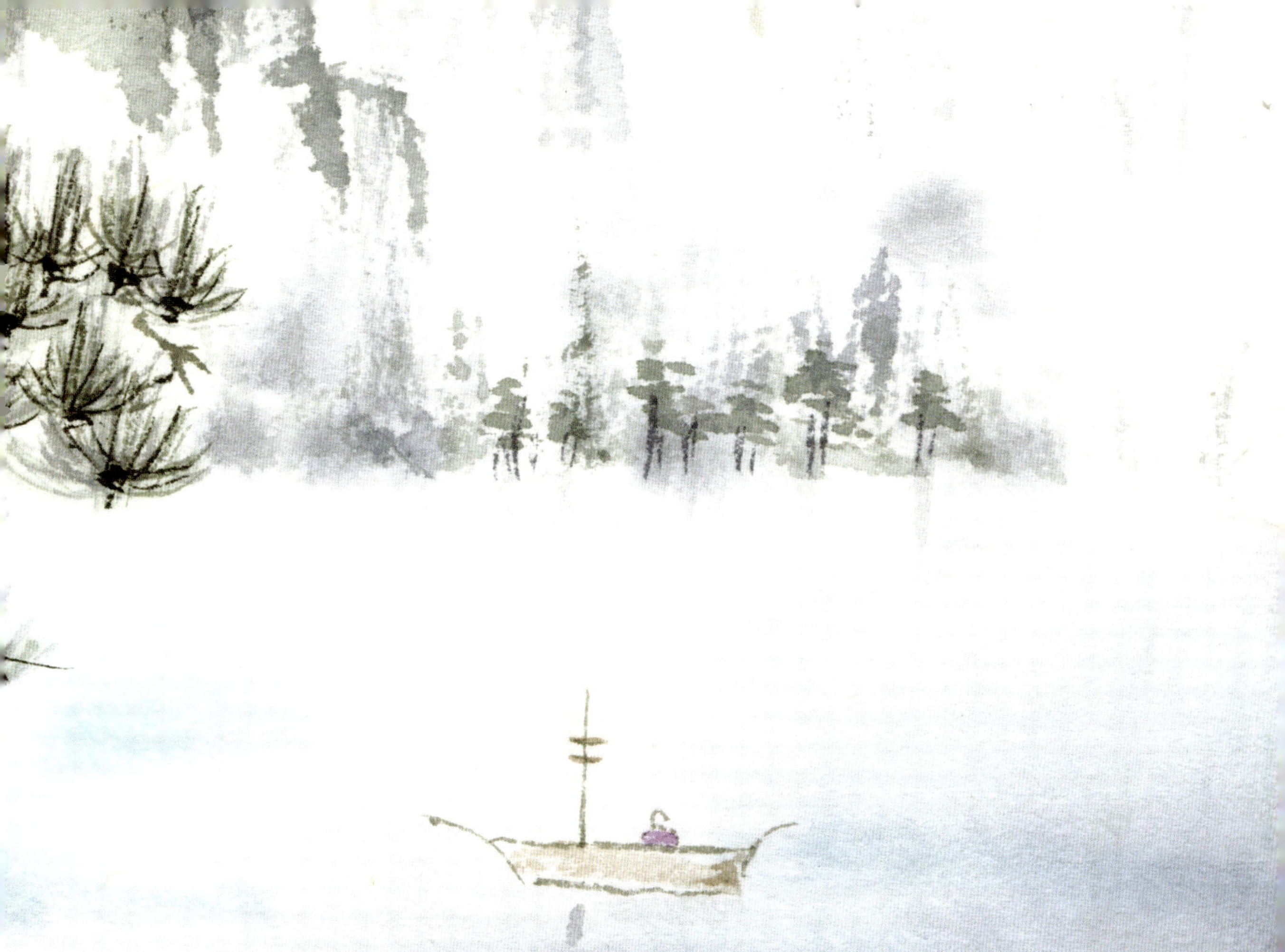

Try this:

Imagine there's a little boat moored to a dock by a lovely lake. Take the person, situation or thing you're distressed about and place it or them in the little boat and untie it. Let the boat find its course in the little lake, no longer your worry.

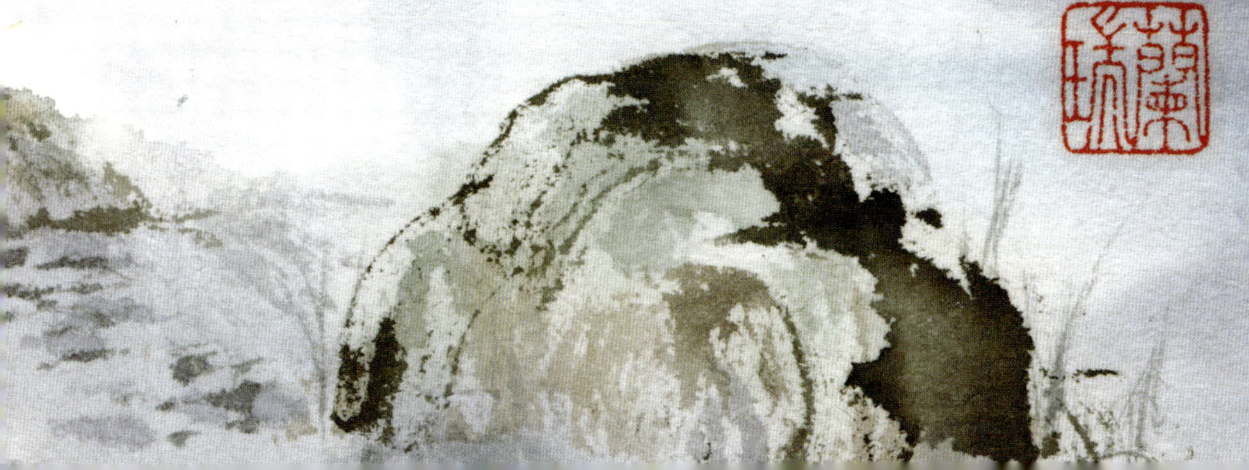

MEDITATION ON

Harmony

When I paint, the work reaches a point that feels harmonious. If I should continue on…it becomes out of harmony and I may have to add a dozen strokes to get it back in harmony.

Johannes Kepler believed that there is a harmony in the cosmos relating to musical sound; while inaudible, it could be heard by the soul and it gave one a feeling of bliss. This is the "music of the spheres."

When I think of Harmony I immediately turn to vocal harmony where there is an underlying chord structure and each singer has his own role. If there is a pitch that is a half-step apart, we sense conflict or uncertainty.

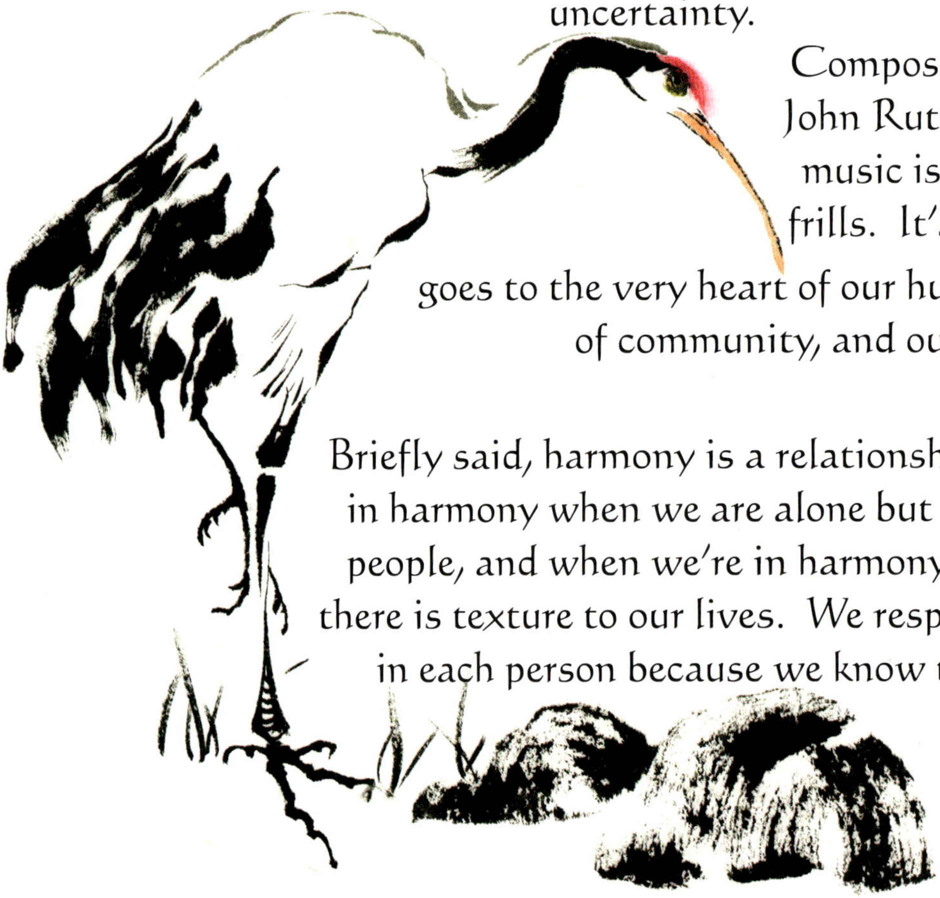

Composer and conductor John Rutter said, "Choral music is not one of life's frills. It's something that goes to the very heart of our humanity, our sense of community, and our souls."

Briefly said, harmony is a relationship. We cannot be in harmony when we are alone but when we're with people, and when we're in harmony we feel a depth, there is texture to our lives. We respect the differences in each person because we know they're needed.

Perhaps in the East the concept is more readily accepted as I have a carved Chinese mood seal that says, "The Harmony of Heaven and Earth." This led me to write a poem about sharing this very harmony with friends in the East, forgetting differences and walking together in the garden of our friendship.

So then... where to start. I think we have to discover our own gift, our raison d' être...our reason of being...the justification of our existence. When we have clarity, knowing our purpose, we see ways to sound our note, and the pleasure of doing this brings so much joy we will continually be open to exactly that. Discord arises when we sound a note that is not authentic, so perhaps always being aware and in the moment will guide us to know when our note is needed.

Paul said it best in Colossians:

Above all, put on love,
which binds everything together
in perfect harmony.

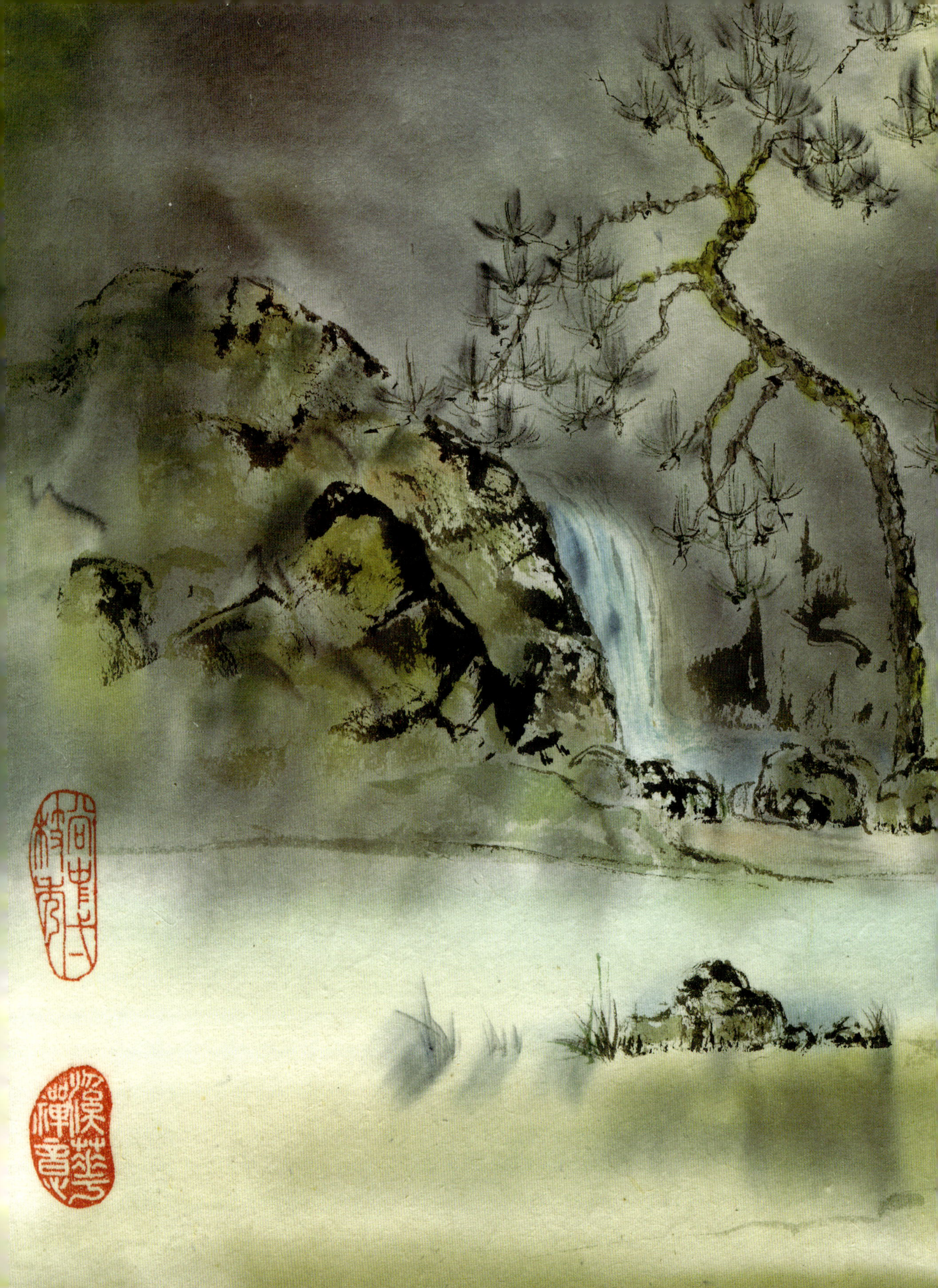

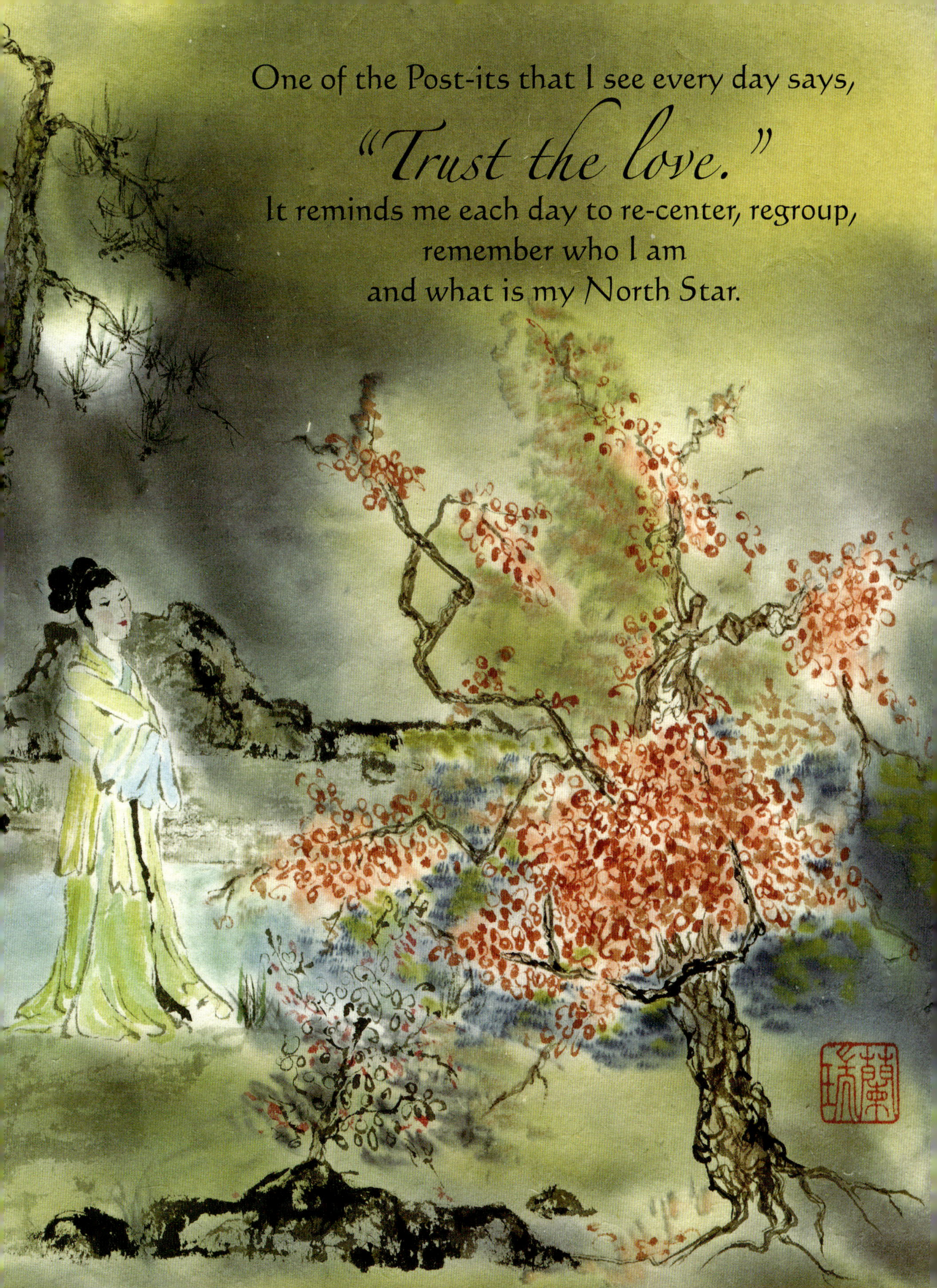
One of the Post-its that I see every day says,
"Trust the love."
It reminds me each day to re-center, regroup,
remember who I am
and what is my North Star.

There was a situation in my life that troubled me greatly for months. One day I felt a peace and an awareness that no matter what happened…

everything was alright and I would be O.K.

The gift of that day opened me up to treasuring being at peace even if I sometimes have to work hard to get there.

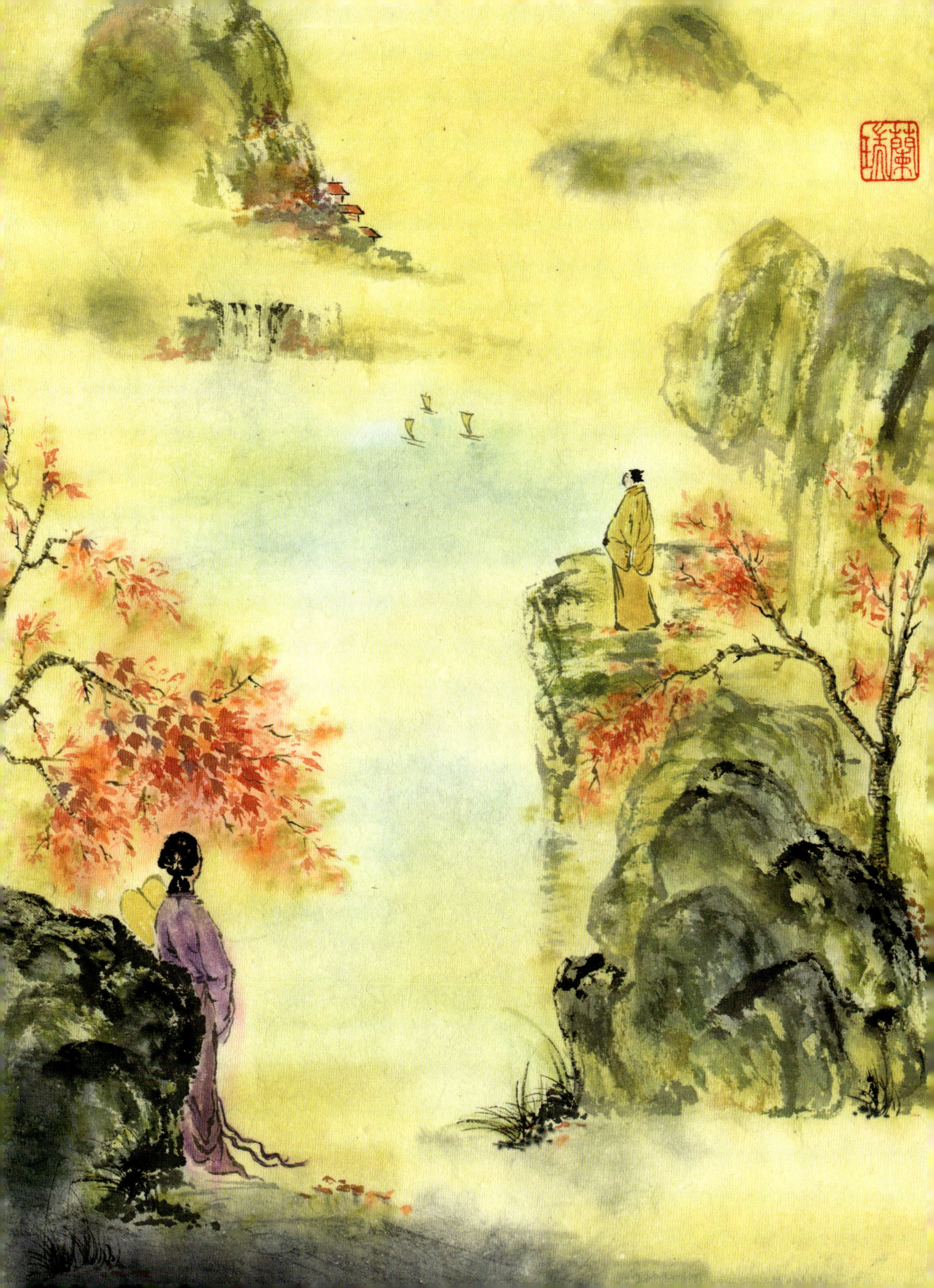

Dr. David Viscott had a similar experience.
He said, "One day he felt a connectedness.
He could feel the presence of each star as a sun in its own right and could feel its heat/energy.
He felt every blade of grass and every leaf as an entity in its own right.
This happened all at the same time, without thinking.

At the same time there was an incredible peace.
He knew that the answer was part of the knowing and he knew that the moment was sacred.
He stood in that state of Grace for about 15 minutes with an enormous sense of Love for everything.
He knew there was no battle and that he had already won.
No matter what would ever happen,
he would turn out O.K."

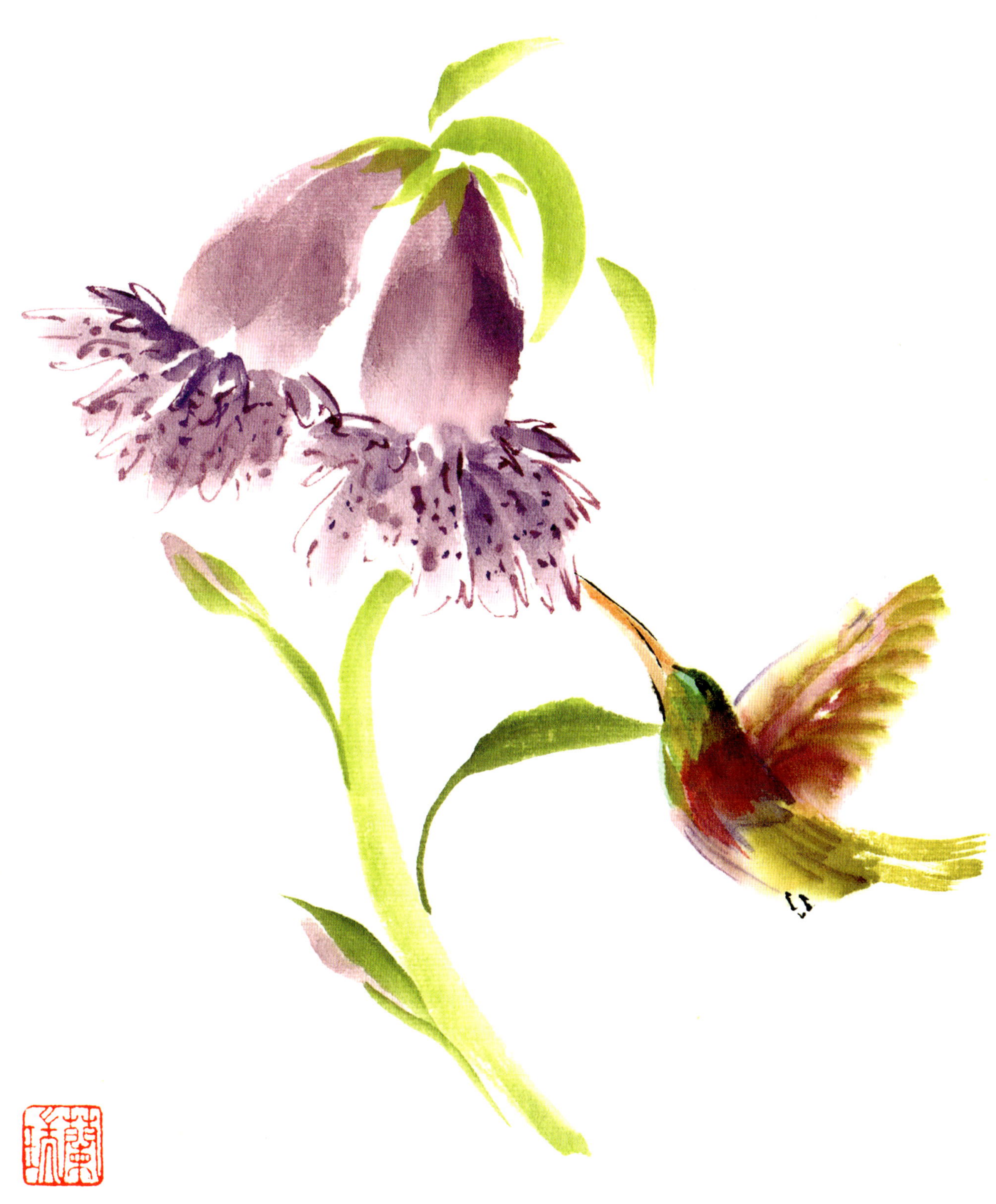

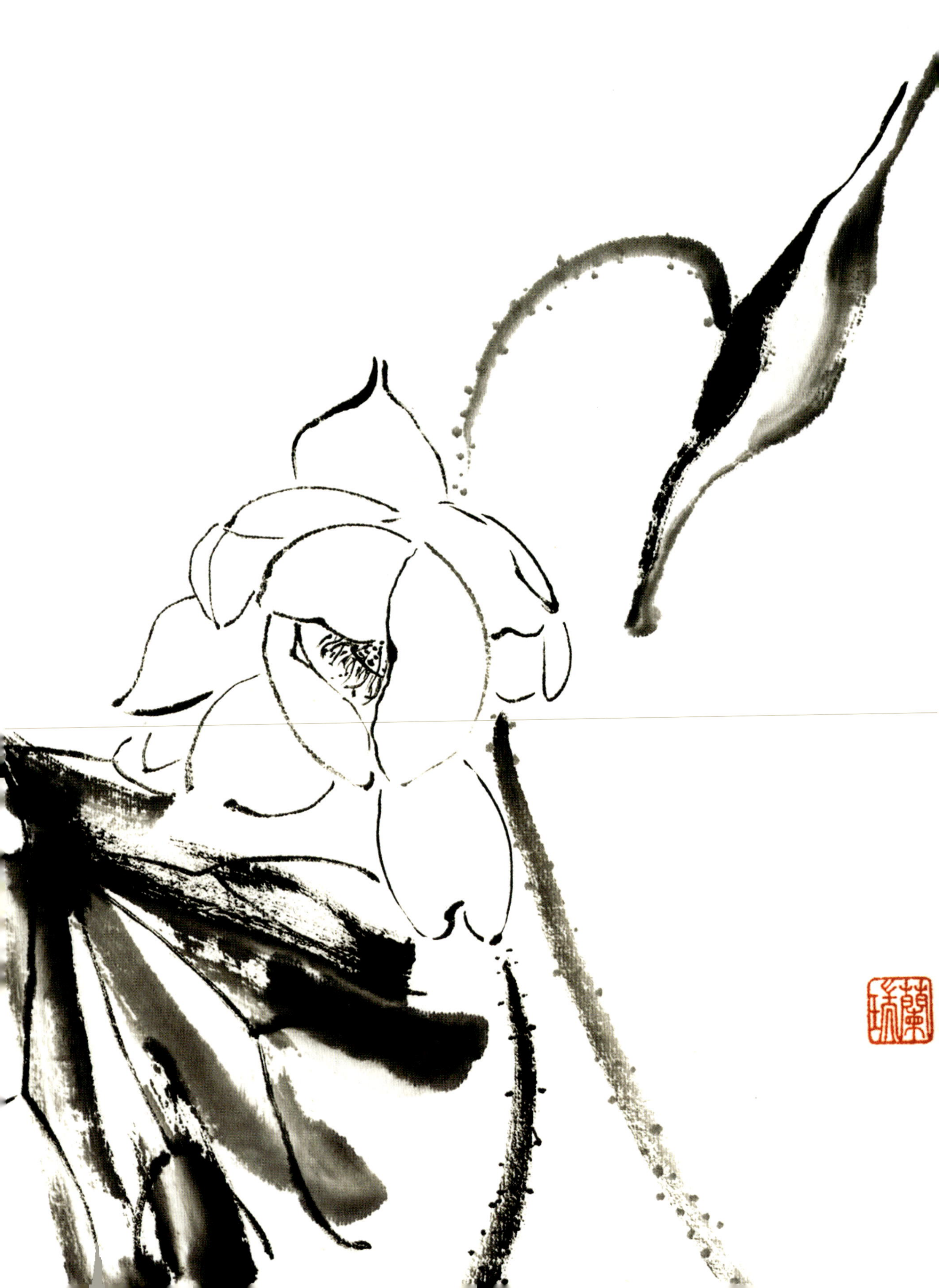

I suppose

surrender is the key.

Being grateful, walking in kindness,
knowing that everything really is out of my control
and having that be a good thing.
It certainly is an anxiety-reliever.

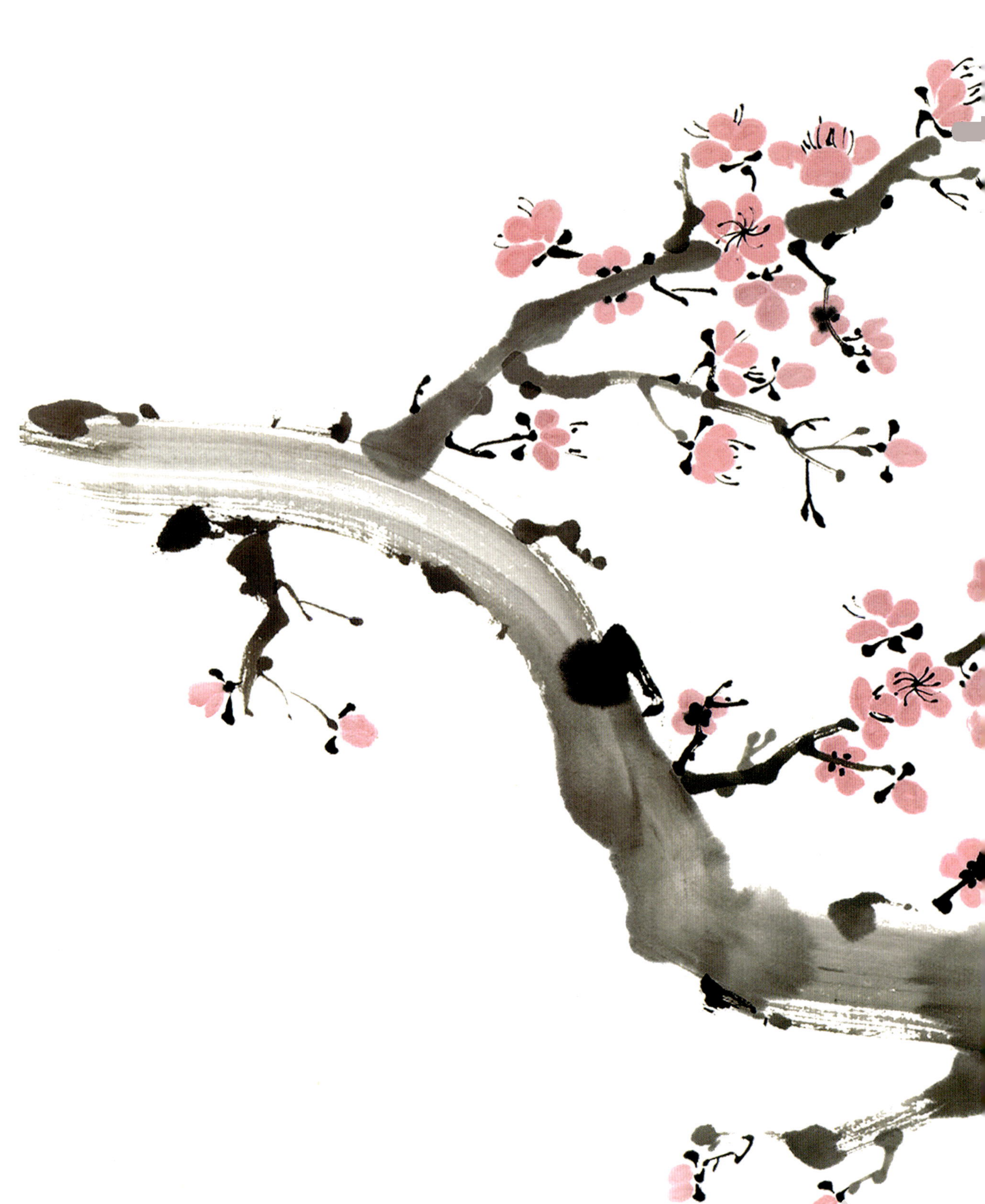

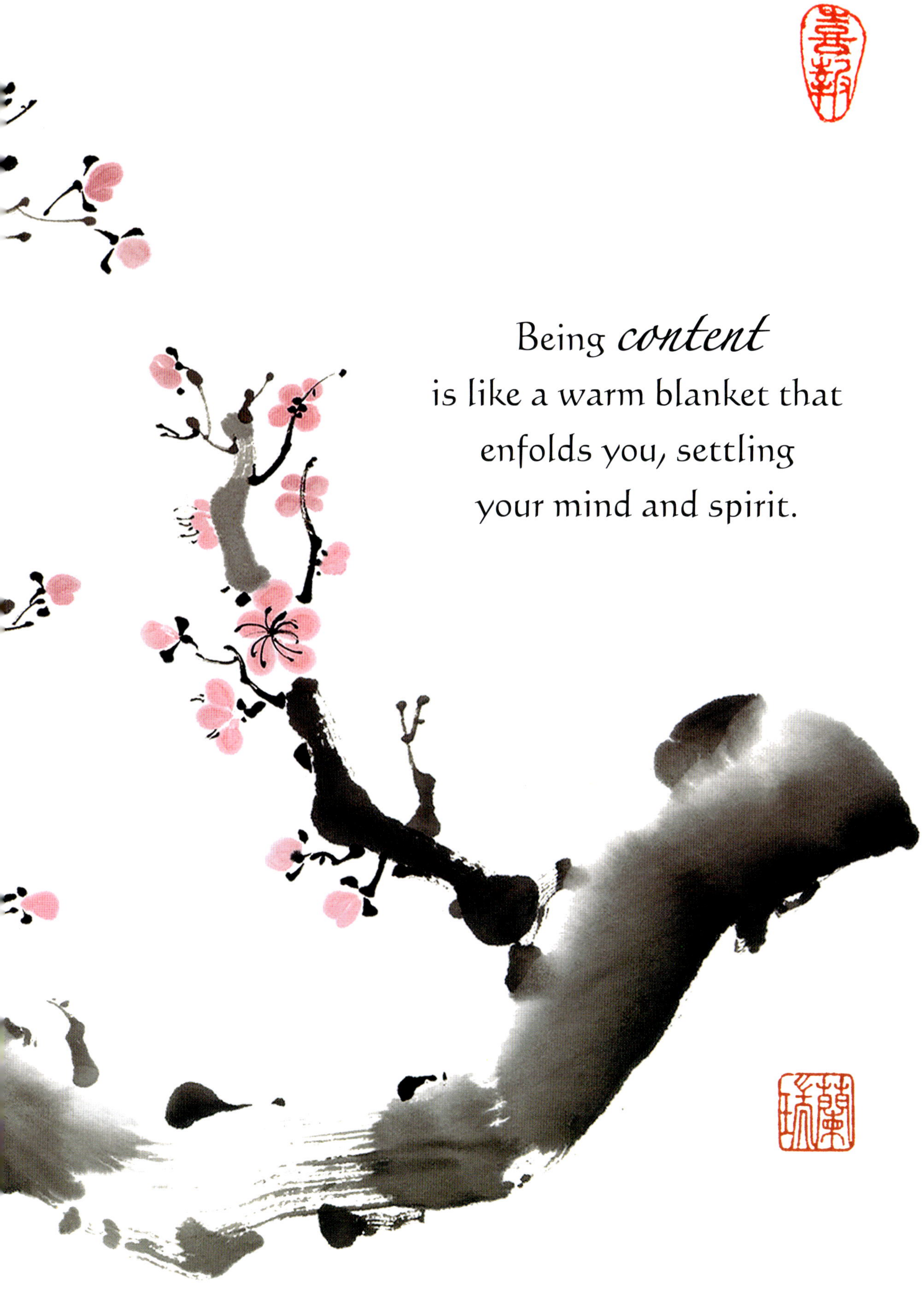

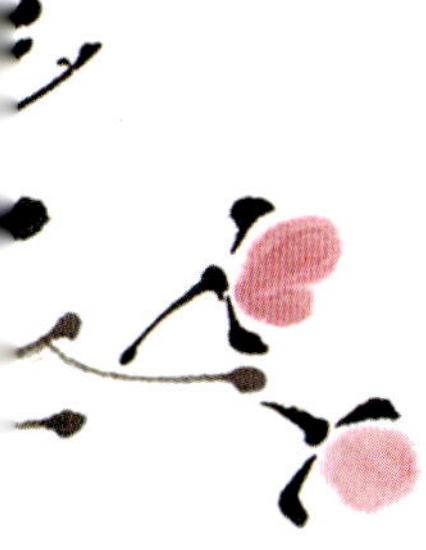

Being *content*
is like a warm blanket that
enfolds you, settling
your mind and spirit.

Pierre Teilhard de Chardin's gift to the world
is the concept of a divine allurement,
calling creation forward to an "Omega Point,"
making the world unified,
meaningful and most of all...hopeful.
In other words, whether we perceive it or not,
the trajectory of humanity tends upward!

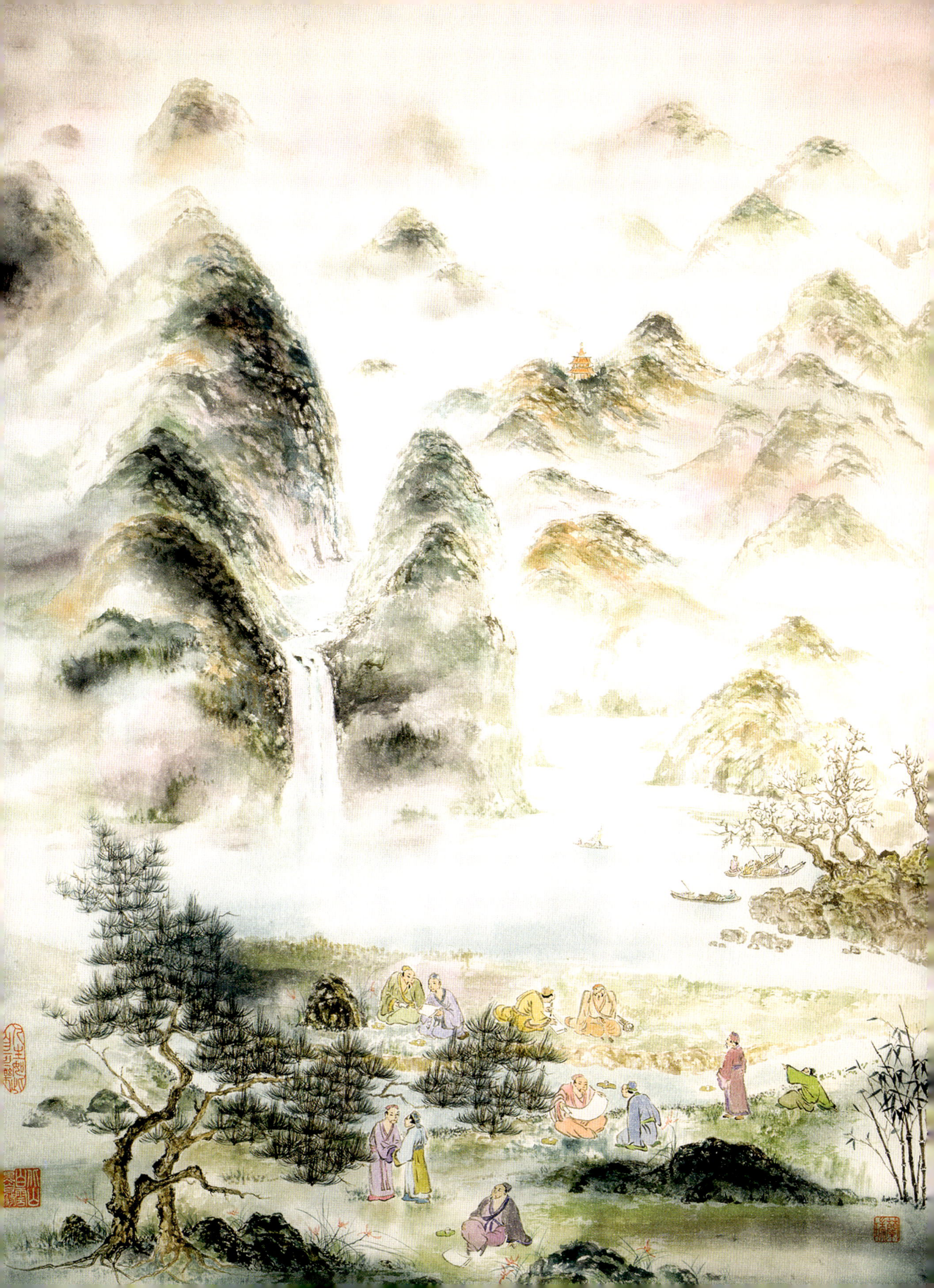

"Love all God's creation,
the whole and every grain of sand in it.
Love every leaf, every ray of God's light.
Love the animals, love the plants, love everything.
If you love everything,
you will perceive the divine mystery in things.
Once you perceive it,
you will begin to understand it better every day.
And you will come at last to love the whole world with an
all-embracing love...
Things flow and are indirectly linked together,
and if you push here, something will move at the other end
of the world. If you strike here, something somewhere will
wince; if you sin here, something somewhere will suffer."

-Fyodor Dostoyevsky, "The Brothers Karamazov"

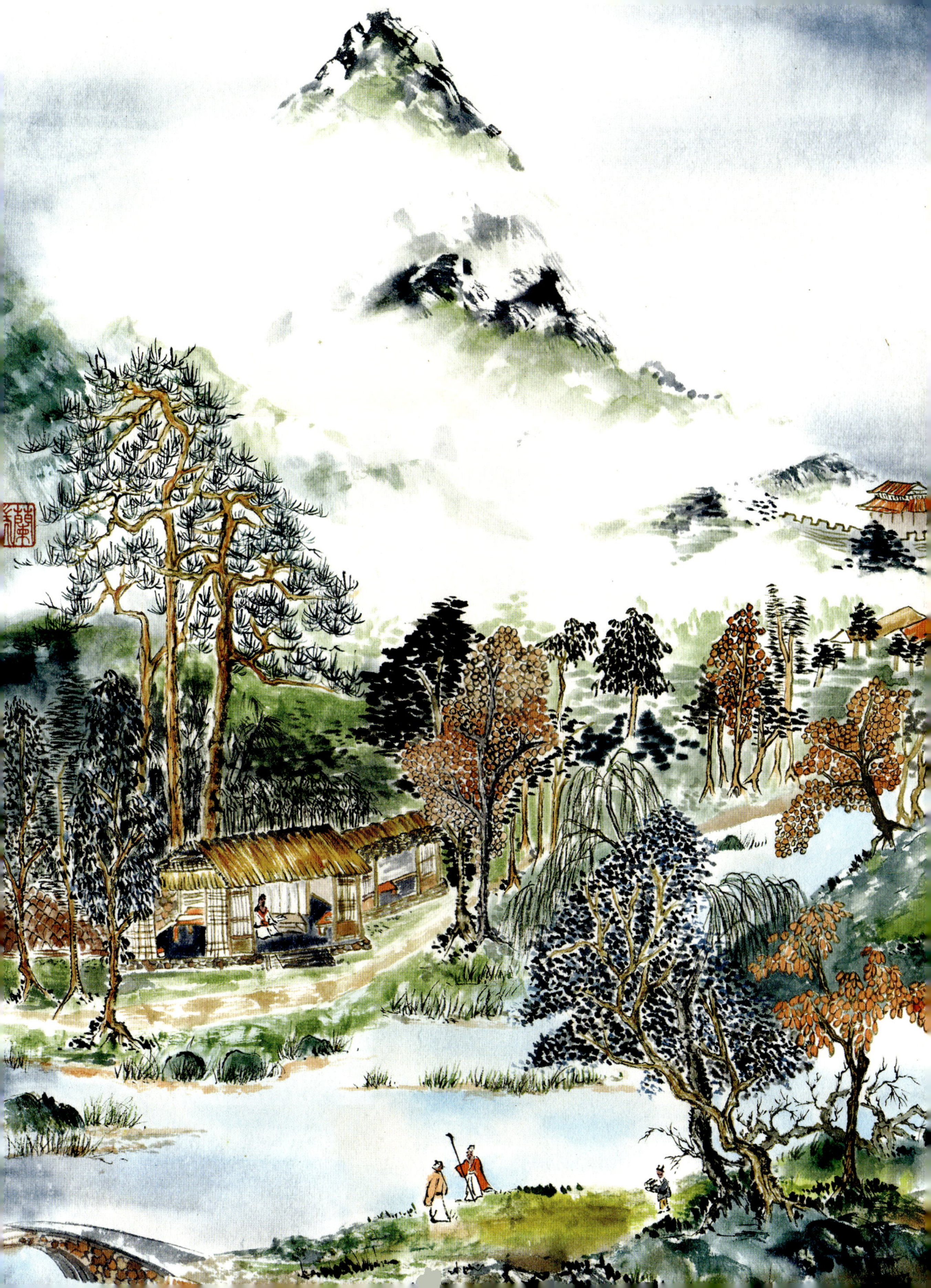

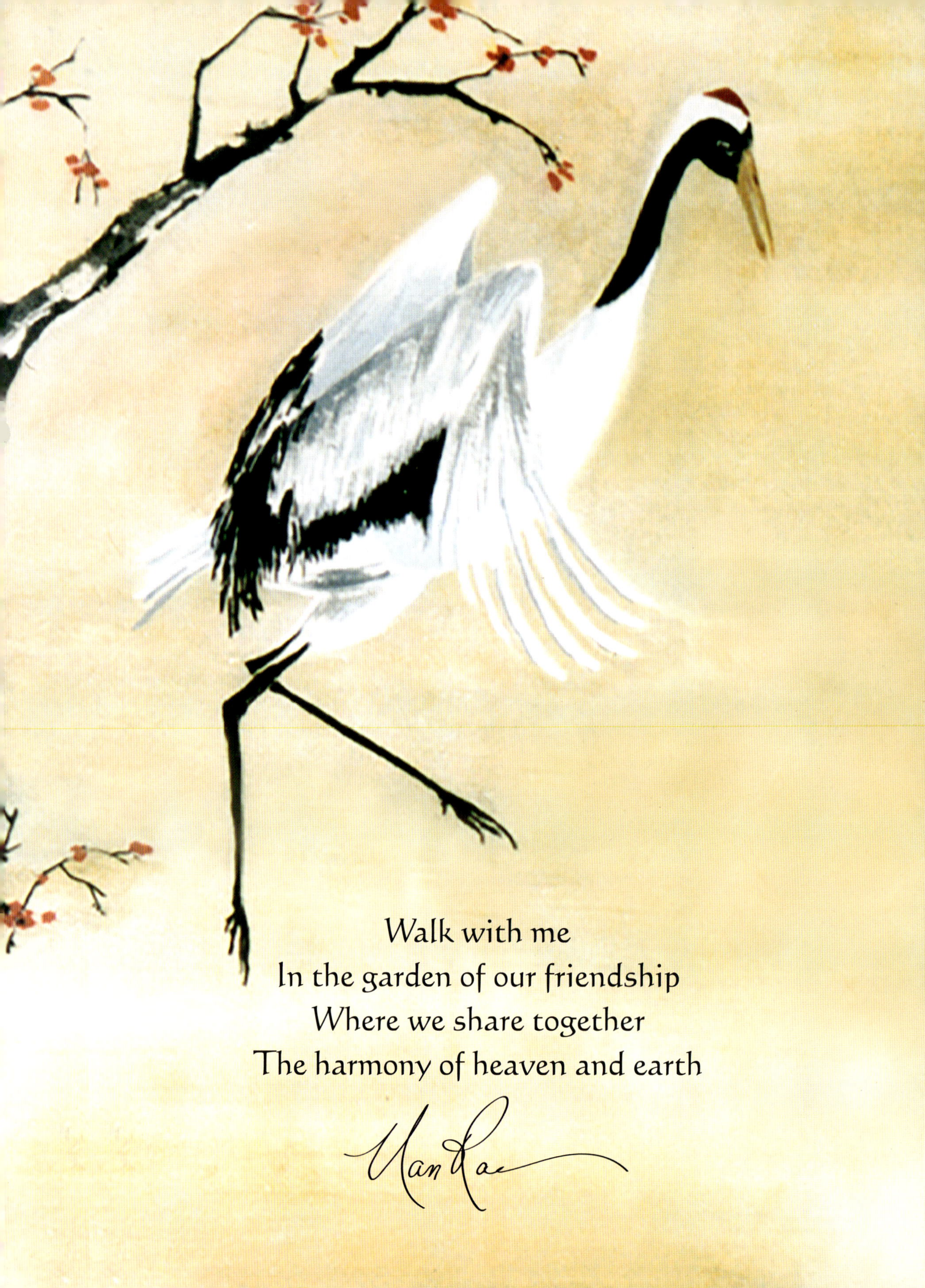
Walk with me
In the garden of our friendship
Where we share together
The harmony of heaven and earth

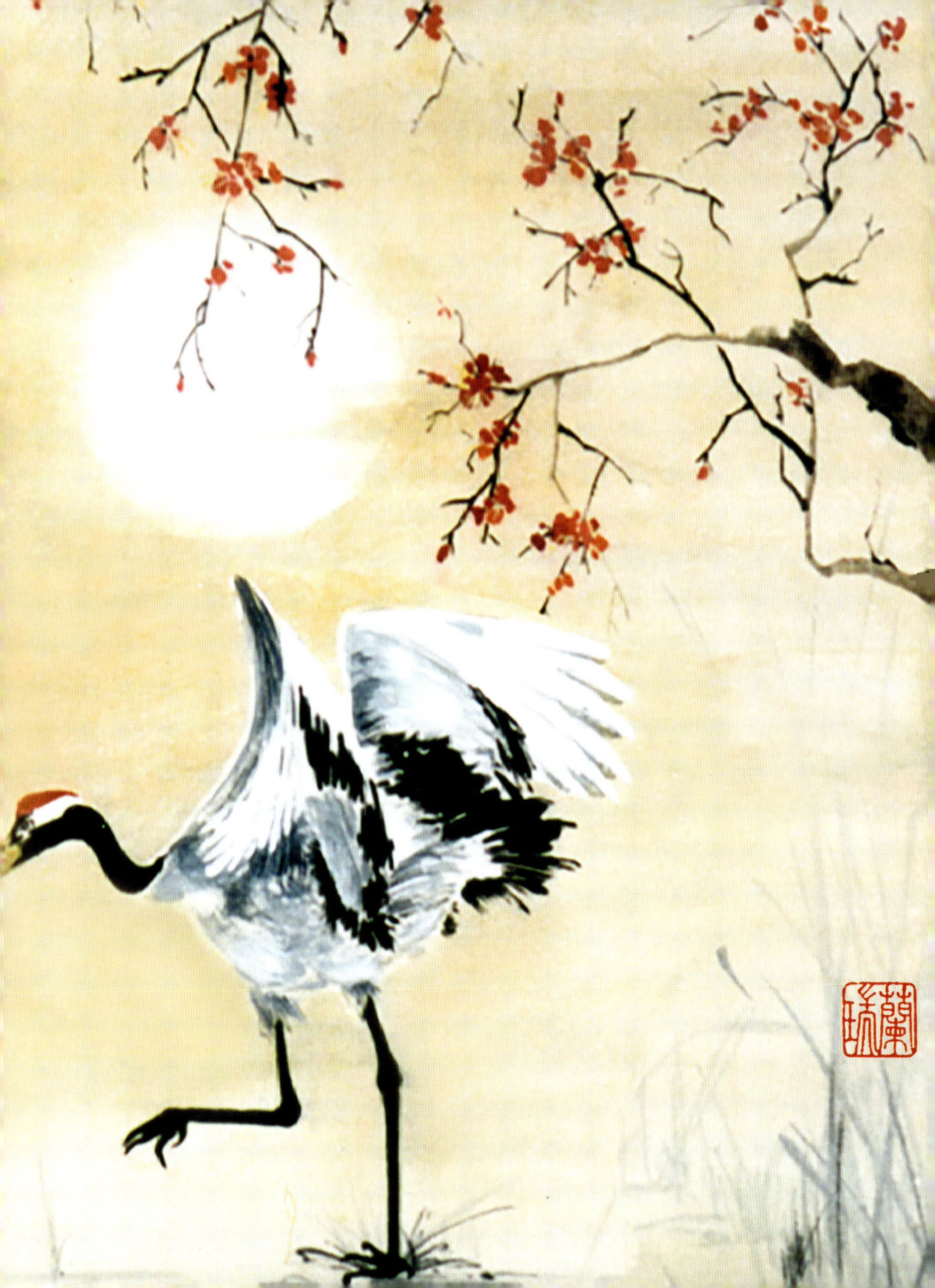

About the Author

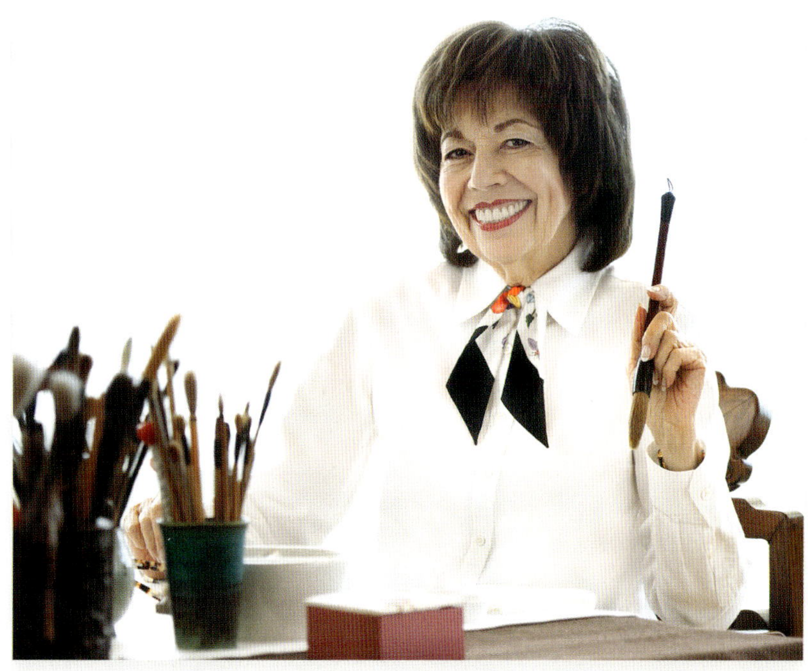

Photo courtesy of **CURTIS**VISION

Nan Rae, author of "What If..." and "That's Just What I Needed Today," is an artist, lecturer, social media influencer living in Southern California. Her Brush Painting classes and book "The Ch'i of the Brush" have inspired thousands. She continues to live by her motto, "Live JOYFULLY!"

Heartfelt thanks to Curtis McElhinney, award winning photographer and videographer for this photo. curtisvision.com

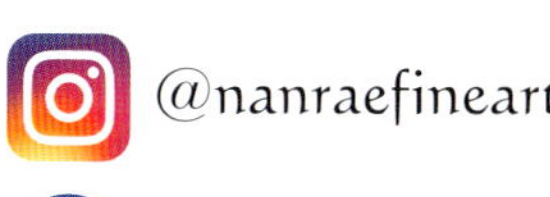

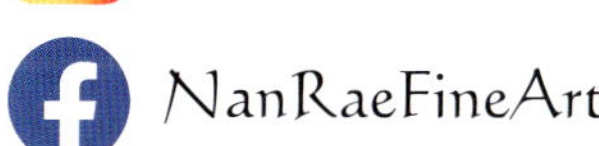

nanraestudio.com

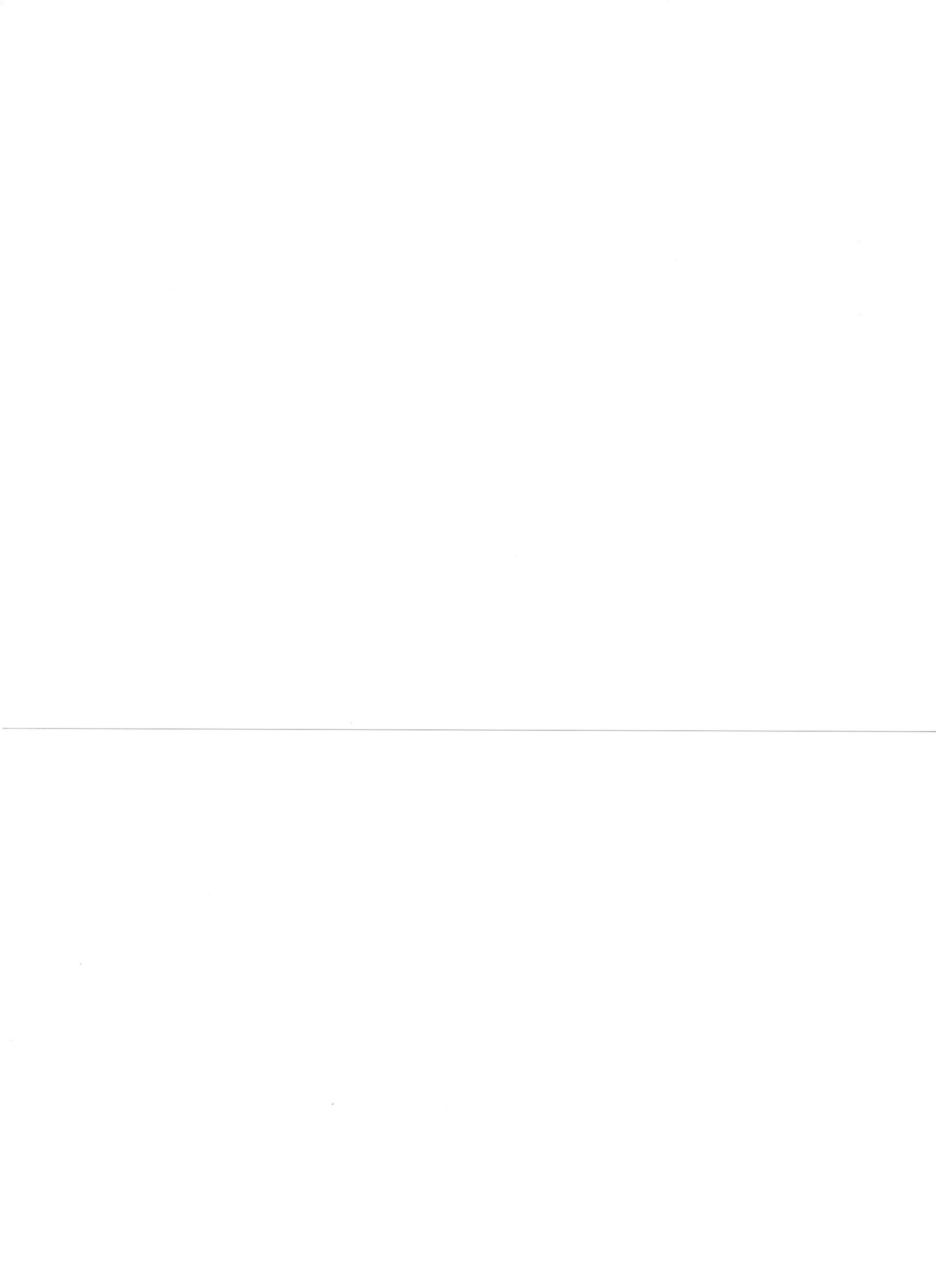